Crested Geckos

Complete Herp Care

Adam Black

1/2023

Crested Gekos

Project Team
Editor: Tom Mazorlig
Copy Editor: Carl Schutt
Cover Design: Cándida Moreira Tómassini
Design Team: Mary Ann Kahn, Patty Escabi

T.F.H. Publications
President/CEO: Glen S. Axelrod
Executive Vice President: Mark E. Johnson
Publisher: Christopher T. Reggio
Production Manager: Kathy Bontz

T.F.H. Publications, Inc.
One TFH Plaza
Third and Union Avenues
Neptune City, NJ 07753

Printed and bound in China
07 08 09   3 5 7 9 8 6 4 2
ISBN 978-0-79382881-4
Library of Congress Cataloging-in-Publication Data
Black, Adam, 1974- Crested geckos : a complete guide to Rhacodactylus / Adam Black.
p. cm.
Includes bibliographical references and index.
ISBN 0-7938-2881-3 (alk. paper)
1. Crested geckos as pets. 2. Rhacodactylus. I. Title.
SF459.G35B53 2005
639.3'952--dc22
2005016725

The Leader In Responsible Animal Care For Over 50 Years!™
www.tfh.com

Table of Contents

My 10 years working for Bill and Marcia Brant, owners of The Gourmet Rodent, Inc., have been an amazing learning experience. The incomparable knowledge gained from my beginnings as a line worker through my advancement to a management position at one of the largest captive reptile breeding facilities in the world has made it possible for me to write this book. I greatly appreciate the encouragement Bill and Marcia have given me in the course of writing this book.

Aside from the owners of the Gourmet Rodent, other fellow staff members helped me out immensely. Thanks to Matt Steen, who supervises the huge crested gecko colony and the team of employees required to keep everything running smoothly. Aside from making my everyday job so much easier, he was a huge help in finding unique specimens to photograph, as well as relating his personal experiences working closely with the crested geckos. Thanks also go to Mike Layman, my fellow co-manager, who was very supportive in the time I was writing the manuscript for this book.

A special thanks to Joe Hiduke, former manager at the Gourmet Rodent. Joe introduced me to the biology and husbandry of the crested geckos when we began building up a colony and continued to help me with information contained within this book after he moved on to bigger and better things. His vast knowledge of reptile biology, captive care, and veterinary techniques has always been invaluable.

To my brother, Jesse Black, whose interest in reptiles clearly rubbed off on me at an early age and undoubtedly solidified my future in herpetoculture. To my mom and recently deceased father who have always been completely supportive in my interests.

And last but certainly not least, thanks to my wife, Susan, and my son, Tyler, who put up with my typing all night long. Susan's encouragement and help in all aspects of writing this book are appreciated greatly.

Over the past two decades, there has been an explosion in the reptile keeping hobby. In the early years, reptiles available from pet stores were typically wild-caught animals that harbored parasites, and little was known about their proper care. Very few vets knew anything about reptile medicine, so most reptiles and amphibians did not survive for long.

As time passed, those with intense interests in herpetology began taking the hobby one step further—providing semi-natural conditions in order to stimulate captive reproduction. This coincided with increased awareness of environmental concerns, including habitat destruction and the resulting extinctions. Captive-bred animals, being healthier and free of parasites, began to be preferable to imported animals. Additionally, with sufficient captive breeding, native populations would not need to be exploited.

As more people began learning how to breed various types of reptiles, new color variations appeared and were mixed in, creating desirable appearances not found naturally. Certain species became popular due to their simple care requirements, calm nature, ease of reproduction, and degree of color and pattern variation. New species became available for experimentation, and some would prove to be very popular. On the lizard front, the leopard gecko, *Eublepharis macularius*, took the reptile world by storm, and was considered to be the perfect pet lizard. Soon, the bearded dragon, *Pogona vitticeps*, was competing for the same title, and though very different from a leopard gecko, it became comparable in terms of meeting

Introduction

the attributes for the perfect pet lizard.

In the heyday of these two species, a newcomer being kept by a handful of dedicated hobbyists was showing promising signs of being a contender to the title of "best pet lizard"—the crested gecko. Compared to the other two species, the crested gecko, *Rhacodactylus ciliatus*, had a most interesting yet alien appearance. It was highly variable in color and proved very simple to keep. Furthermore, it was very easy to breed, and the females laid a large number of clutches per season.

This species had just been rediscovered in the tropical rainforests of the New Caledonian archipelago after it was assumed to be extinct for many years. Due to this rarity factor and the species' uniqueness and irresistible charm, initial captive-produced crested geckos sold for great amounts of money. As more and more people found out how easy it was to breed this interesting gecko, the price dropped as captive-produced hatchlings became more available. Even those that were uneasy about reptiles could become fascinated by these non-menacing, delightfully odd creatures.

Today, the crested gecko continues to gain popularity. No longer are they only available from specialty breeders, as many local pet stores regularly have them in stock. As more are bred, new intense colors and bold patterns continue to surface. The future continues to look promising for crested geckos and the other species of *Rhacodactylus*, as their rising popularity and widespread captive breeding help make sure these unique animals do not become extinct.

Chapter 1

Natural History

Although nearly all the crested geckos and other *Rhacodactylus* are bred in captivity, they cannot be considered domestic animals. They still have their natural instincts intact. Like other reptiles—and wild animals in general—these geckos have adapted to live in certain environmental conditions. To better understand your gecko's behavior and its habitat requirements, it is helpful to know about its natural history.

Range and Habitat

New Caledonia is a small group of islands located northeast of Australia, about halfway between Australia and Fiji. Long inhabited by Melanesian people, it is now a French territory that, with combined land area, is slightly smaller than the state of New

Crested geckos and the other *Rhacodactylus* inhabit the warm humid forests of New Caledonia.

Jersey. It is located just north of the Tropic of Cancer, so the islands have a humid tropical climate influenced by the southeast trade winds.

The main island of New Caledonia, known as Grande Terre, is a long narrow strip of land with a central backbone of a mountain range, skirted with coastal plains. Off the southern end of Grande Terre is the Ile des Pins (Isle of Pines), named for the abundance of conifers there. Several other tiny islands are found off the coasts of these two larger islands, many of which are also inhabited by *Rhacodactylus* species. Another group of small islands, the Loyalty Islands, lie just to the northeast, but no *Rhacodactylus* species have been found there.

Crested geckos are known from the southern third of Grande Terre, as well as isolated populations on the Isle of Pines and a nearby small island. There, they occupy primary forests where they live an arboreal lifestyle, especially in smaller trees and large shrubs. They are nocturnal, active during the nighttime and spending the day coiled up in the foliage of these small trees. Other species coexist in the same range and habitat as crested geckos, but some live in other parts of Grande Terre where cresteds haven't been found.

The "Giant Geckos" of the Genus *Rhacodactylus*

The members of the genus *Rhacodactylus* are sometimes referred to as "giant geckos." This name doesn't necessarily apply to all of the six species within the genus, though. The largest species, *Rhacodactylus leachianus*, is also the largest of all living gecko species. It can grow to a total length of 17 inches (43.2 cm). The second largest species of the genus, *Rhacodactylus trachyrhyncus*, grows to about 13 inches (33 cm). The remaining species of *Rhacodactylus* average between 8 and 10 inches (20.3 and 25.4 cm).

Gargantuan Geckos

Though *Rhacodactylus leachianus* is considered the largest living gecko, there is still the possibility that the New Zealand native *Hoplodactylus delcourti* is still alive. This giant grew to at least 20 inches total length. Unless more living specimens of this giant gecko are discovered, it is presumed to be extinct. The few specimens preserved in museums are all that are known of this giant gecko. There are several other large geckos approaching the size of *R. leachianus*, including the giant leaf-tail gecko, *Uroplatus fimbriatus*, and the tokay gecko, *Gekko gecko*, both growing to about 14 inches total length.

All members of the genus *Rhacodactylus* are found only in New Caledonia. Aside from the variance in size, the species all vary in appearance. One unique feature they all have in common is the presence of a flattened tail tip with adhesive lamellae (a series of fine ridges) on the underside, similar to those found on the underside of their toes. This "extra finger," along with a prehensile tail, help the various types of *Rhacodactylus* in their travels through vegetation. Another common name applied to species of *Rhacodactylus* is prehensile-tailed geckos, which is more accurate than giant geckos.

All giant geckos are omnivores, eating both plant and animal material. They will eat nearly any animal they can capture, including insects, spiders, snails, and even small lizards, birds, and rodents. Some can even be cannibalistic, feeding on younger, smaller individuals of the same species. They also consume soft fruits, including figs from the native species of *Ficus* trees, as well as other native berry-like fruits. They will also consume flowers and the nectar and pollen they contain. They possibly serve as pollinators for certain species of plants.

While five of the six species of *Rhacodactylus* are oviparous (egg-laying), one species, *Rhacodactylus trachyrhyncus*, is

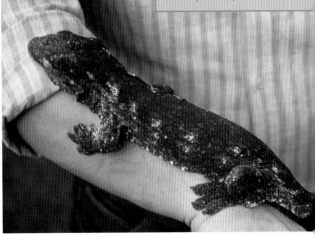

The New Caledonian giant gecko is likely the largest living gecko, occasionally reaching a length of 17 inches (43.2 cm).

unusual in that it is viviparous, giving birth to live young. All egg-laying species normally lay two eggs per clutch, and R. *trachyrhynchus* gives birth to two neonates at a time.

All species are arboreal, spending most of their lives up in trees. Several species may occupy the same area of forest, but the different species may frequent different levels of the trees. R. *leachianus* and R. *trachyrhynchus* prefer the high canopy of the rainforest, while R. *ciliatus*, R. *chahoua*, and R. *sarasinorum* prefer the middle to lower levels of the trees. R. *auriculatus* seems to prefer a different habitat, being more likely to be found in the low vegetation of drier open woodlands or scrub habitats, though it can occasionally be found in rainforests.

Crested geckos tend to inhabit shrubs and the lower branches of trees, rather than living high in the canopy.

Taxonomy

Beginning with Carl Linnaeus in 1758 and continuing today, taxonomy (literally "law of arrangement") is a field of biology that attempts to organize all living things by similar features to identify evolutionary relationships.

Crested geckos are classified as follows:

> Kingdom: Animalia (animals)
>
> Phylum: Chordata (possessing a spinal cord)
>
> Subphylum: Vertebrata (possessing a backbone)
>
> Class: Reptilia (Reptiles)
>
> Order: Squamata (Snakes and Lizards)
>
> Suborder: Sauria (Lizards)
>
> Infraorder: Gekkota (Geckos)
>
> Family: Diplodactylidae (Australian and Oceanic Geckos)
>
> Genus: *Rhacodactylus*
>
> Species: *ciliatus*

This taxonomical organization is subject to debate, depending on the research one agrees with. Continued studies of this genus and its relatives will prove or disprove the current models of classification. For example, the genus *Rhacodactylus* was included in the family Gekkonidae, but it is now generally agreed upon that they belong in the family Diplodactylidae, though there are those who disagree.

Every animal described by a member of the scientific community is given a scientific name, which is normally in Latin. The scientific name includes the genus and species. When writing the genus and species, it is always in italics, and the first letter of the genus name is always capitalized, and the first letter of the species is always in lowercase.

Common names, which are used more often outside of the scientific community, are not used scientifically due to a variety of localized names which creates confusion between colleagues around the world. These names are of course easier to remember, and, like scientific names, often descriptive in the local language. Crested geckos were originally known as "Guichenot's giant gecko," though once popularized by reptile keepers, other more descriptive names emerged, including eyelash gecko, crested giant gecko, and New Caledonian crested gecko, but just crested gecko has become the most accepted name in the reptile keeping community.

What's in a Name?

The crested gecko was first described in 1866 by the French naturalist Guichenot, who gave it the name *Correlophus ciliatus*. It was later moved to the genus *Rhacodactylus*, but it retained its descriptive species name. *Rhacodactylus* curiously translates to "axis or backbone finger," and most likely relates to the shape of their toes. The actual toe is slender, and is sharply raised up from the underlying flat adhesive toe pads, giving each toe a ridge, or "backbone." The species name *ciliatus* means "eyelash or hairy," which of course refers to the double rows of spiny scales forming "eyelashes" and extending down the head, neck, and back.

The genus *Rhacodactylus* has a total of six species. These are *Rhacodactylus auriculatus* (gargoyle gecko), *R. chahoua* (Bavay's giant gecko or mossy prehensile-tailed gecko), *R. ciliatus* (crested gecko), *R. leachianus* (giant gecko), *R. sarasinorum* (Roux's giant gecko or slender prehensile-tailed gecko), and *R. trachyrhynchus* (rough-snouted gecko).

Two of these species are further divided into two subspecies based on drastic differences in appearance or habits. The subspecies of *R. leachianus* are *R. leachianus leachianus* and *R. leachianus henkeli*. *R. trachyrhynchus* is also divided into two subspecies: *R. trachyrhynchus trachyrhynchus* and *R. trachyrhynchus trachycephalus*. As more research is done, additional subspecies may be named for these and other species.

Crested Geckos: Discovery and Research

After Guichenot's formal description of *Rhacodactylus ciliatus* in 1866, there were still no detailed studies of this species in its native habitat. Time passed, and little attention was paid to this species until recently, when herpetoculture became more popular. European keepers began experimenting with other *Rhacodactylus* species that became sporadically available as imports, and gradually the American keepers caught on. Yet, crested geckos remained to be rediscovered and never showed up in the pet trade.

Crested geckos are sometimes called eyelash geckos because of the fringe of scales above their eyes.

Searching the areas of New Caledonia where preserved museum specimens were collected failed to turn up any individuals. Due to lack of reports of this species for such an extended period of time, some assumed that this species may have become extinct because of human activity on the islands.

Then, in 1994, the species was found alive on the Isle de Pins, off the southeast coast of Grand Terre. An expedition led by Wilhelm Henkel and Robert Seipp resulted in additional specimens found on the island, and Philippe de Vosjoli and Frank Fast also found the species and legally brought some back to the United States. Recognizing the opportunity, smugglers illegally exported more crested geckos out of New Caledonia, which all eventually contributed to the founding stock for all of the geckos in captivity today. More recently, the crested gecko has been found at several locations in the southern third of Grand Terre.

Herp Is the Word

Throughout this book, you will see the term *herp*. This word refers to both reptiles and amphibians together. Herp comes from the word *herpetology,* which is the study of reptiles and amphibians. When speaking about the hobby of keeping reptiles and amphibians, you can call it the *herp hobby. Herpetoculture* is the keeping and breeding of reptiles and amphibians. A *herper* is someone who participates in the herp hobby or herpetoculture (also called a *herp hobbyist*).

The initial animals that became available were very expensive. Those who recognized the potential of this new type of lizard and attempted to propagate this species found that they were easy to care for and very prolific. These qualities, combined with their alien appearance and multitude of colors, quickly took the ever-growing reptile industry by storm. As more and more were produced, prices began to drop, and seemingly infinite combinations of colors and patterns began to appear. Selective breeding began to emphasize some of these traits, the results of which helped make the crested gecko even more popular. Soon, commercial breeders and hobbyists were producing a combined total of tens of thousands of crested geckos per year.

Features of the Crested Gecko

Adult crested geckos are heavy bodied and plump, with proportionally large heads. Legs are stout, and the flaps of skin running along the back side of the thighs make the legs look even thicker than they actually are. Just past the eyes, the head broadens greatly, creating the

The wide crest on the head and neck give the crested gecko its most common name. This individual is a red dalmatian crested gecko.

wide triangular head, further accentuated with the spiny scales. Head width and overall heftiness seem to vary between individuals, yet don't appear to be an indicator of sex, as they are in other species of lizards.

The Crests

The crested gecko's popularity is partially based on its distinctive appearance. The most notable feature is the pair of crests that gives the gecko its common names. These are ridges of skin edged with pointed scales that begin over the eye and extend around the broad, triangular crown of the head and down the back of the neck. The crests usually disappear in the upper back region, though some have a crest that continues to the base of the tail. The pointed scales above the eye give the gecko the appearance of having eyelashes, which accounts for its other common name, the eyelash gecko. These scales above the eyes sometimes point upwards on some individuals, while they point outward in others. The function of the spiny crests, combined with the proportionally large and broad head, may make the gecko appear too unappetizing to potential predators, though this is purely speculative.

The Toes

The crested gecko has several adaptations for climbing in the trees. Like other climbing geckos, *Rhacodactylus* species have specialized pads on the underside of their toes. These pads are composed of millions of tiny hair-like structures called lamellae that interact at a the atomic level to grant the gecko adhesive ability. This even allows the geckos to effortlessly climb smooth surfaces, such as glass. The toes also have webbing between them, and small claws at

Eyes Without Lids

Though some species of geckos have eyelids (the family Eublepharidae), *Rhacodactylus* species do not. The lids of their eyes are fused into one transparent scale, called a brille or spectacle. This scale protects the eye and keeps it from dehydrating. It is shed along with the rest of the skin. In order to keep their eyes free of debris, *Rhacodactylus* must clean their eyes by licking them with their tongues.

their tips. Some keepers will develop an irritation from allowing crested geckos to climb on soft skin, due to the way the lamellae and claws adhere to the skin. These effects are not long lasting and are of little discomfort.

The Senses

The large, round eyes of New Caledonian geckos are adapted for their nocturnal lifestyle, with a vertical pupil that can dilate depending on light levels. The pupil will appear as a thin slit during brightly lit conditions to minimize the amount of light entering the eye. In the dark, the gecko's pupil will open much wider. A close examination of the iris will reveal a complex pattern of tiny veins and pigmentation.

A crested gecko's sense of taste is so well developed that some individuals seem to show preferences toward certain flavors of fruit puree. It is assumed that a crested gecko uses its sense of smell to find fruits to feed on. Its large eyes are good at detecting motion, which may be why fast-moving insects like crickets are eagerly chased down, while slow-moving mealworms are often ignored.

Crested geckos have a pair of ear openings on either side of the head. Inside is a tympanum that picks up sound vibrations. There are reports of crested geckos making sounds, but this is infrequent and usually only occurs during fights. This species is definitely not as vocal as other species of geckos, such as tokay geckos.

As a gecko is exploring new terrain, it will often lick the surface it is walking on with its tongue. Most likely, the gecko will be picking up chemical messages from other geckos that have been in the vicinity and can use these pheromonal trails to track down potential mates, follow commonly used pathways, and avoid the territory of rival males.

Rhacodactylus, like many reptiles, have a well-developed Jacobson's organ, also known as the vomeronasal organ. This is located in the roof of the mouth and functions by sensing its environment similar to smelling or tasting. Geckos can often be seen licking their surroundings, especially when traveling in new locations. When their tongue comes in contact with a surface, it picks up various scent molecules. The tongue is then brought back into the mouth, where the Jacobson's organ can then analyze the molecules. It can then recognize certain "scents" as pheromones from potential nearby mates, markings left by rival males, and may be able to recognize the presence of potential predators, food, etc.

Because they have no eyelids, *Rhacodactylus* (*R. leachianus* pictured here) must clean their eyes with their tongue.

The Tail

The crested gecko has a somewhat prehensile tail that it can use to hold on to branches for support. On the underside of the tail tip is a pad of lamellae similar to that found on the toes. The clinging ability of the tail lamellae is clearly felt when handling a crested gecko.

Many gecko species have plump tails, due to the fat reserves contained within. Crested geckos do not store significant amounts of fat in their tail, and it is very slender compared to some other types of geckos.

Crested geckos will lose their tails very easily. Rough handling, grasping the tail, and breeding may result in loss of the tail. Aside from the tail being broken off, the geckos are able to voluntarily shed their tails when they feel threatened, which is known as autotomy. Many other types of geckos have fracture planes between each of

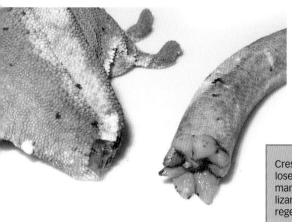

Crested geckos will easily lose their tails, but unlike many other species of lizards, they do not regenerate them.

Champion Jumpers

Crested geckos have the ability to leap off a branch or hand and land safely on the ground far below without injury. To assure a safe landing, this species has webbing between their rear legs and the base of the tail. When jumping, the gecko spreads his legs out to extend the webbing to glide outward. Then, the leg webbing, with the additional help of extended toe webbing, is used to parachute to a soft landing. A gecko sitting motionless on one's hand will catch the handler off guard when he unexpectedly takes a leap to the floor.

the tail bones, allowing for easy detachment without loosing the entire tail. The missing tail tip would then gradually be regenerated. Crested geckos only have one fracture plane at the base of the tail, and do not have the ability to regenerate the tail. It is reported that very few crested geckos observed in the wild have intact tails, yet captive specimens missing tails are considered by most to be undesirable.

The ability to lose the entire tail, along with the inability to regenerate it, leads to questions on as to why this adaptation exists. With other geckos that regenerate their tails, they have numerous opportunities in their life to use the defensive trick of dropping their tail to elude assailants. Crested geckos get one chance, and afterward that defensive strategy is unavailable to them. One idea is that the tail is only necessary for balance in the slender juvenile stage, and it becomes unnecessary as the gecko matures into a stockier build. The fact that the tail has lamellae and is clearly used for grasping onto branches indicates that it serves a purpose at least at some point in its life.

Further research is necessary in order to understand the function of tails other than for balance and defensive autotomy. This may even shed light on causes of poorly understood tail problems commonly seen in captive specimens, especially kinked pelvises, kinked tails, and floppy tail syndrome, which is commonly blamed on nutritional problems, although this has not been proven.

The Mouth

Members of this species have relatively large mouths when compared to other geckos of similar size. Their jaws are lined with many small teeth, all of about the same size. They are capable of biting in defense, though to humans this will consist of a pinch, and most likely won't be able to break the skin.

The lamellae on the toes of cresteds and other geckos allow them climb almost any surface—including glass.

Skin-eating Geckos

Don't be alarmed if you see your crested gecko with pieces of skin hanging out of its mouth. Many geckos, including the New Caledonian geckos, eat their shed skin after or during the shedding process. There are several theories explaining this behavior. The two most accepted are that the geckos are reclaiming certain nutrients and that they are preventing predators from following their trail.

Size

A full-grown adult crested gecko will measure between 8 to 9 inches (20.3 to 22.9 cm) total length, including the tail if present. Without the tail, the body length (snout-to-vent length or SVL) is about 4.5 inches (11.4 cm). They can weigh up to 2.3 ounces (65 g), though most average less. Baby crested geckos hatch out at about 3 inches (7.6 cm) total length, and weight about 1/20 of an ounce (1.5 g).

Skin

Crested geckos have skin that is covered with tiny granular scales. Though the skin of adults often has a rough appearance, it is actually quite smooth and silky feeling. Even the spiny scales on the crests are in no way sharp or prickly. Though the skin is not thick, it is tough and resistant to abrasion.

Like all reptiles, *Rhacodactylus* species have to shed their skin in order to grow. This process is known as ecdysis. When a gecko is preparing to shed its skin, the old dead outer layers of skin will detach from the underlying new skin, initially giving the gecko a dull, somewhat milky coloration. The gecko will then begin to tear its skin off using his mouth and feet, and will then eat the shed skin. The primary purpose for eating shed skin is most likely a defensive strategy. If pieces of shed skin were left behind, a trail would be made for predators to follow to the source.

Coloration Another feature of crested gecko skin is the variety and patterning of pigmentation. The color of this species can range from varying shades

One trait that has made crested geckos popular with breeders is the great variability in color and pattern present in the species.

of dull brown or gray to unexpectedly bright colors of yellow and red. Some individuals will be of only one color, while others will have lighter colored patterning or highlights. When present, this contrasting light coloration will usually emphasize the spiny scales of the crests, and where the crest diminishes on the upper back, a lightly broken wide stripe will continue the length of the back and down the tail. Those lacking this patterning will often still have light marking on the top surface of the tail. Either type (normally called *morphs* by herpetoculturists) may also have light striping on the edges of the rear leg webbing, and on the postanal tubercle, the large bump on both sides of the tail base. Darker markings are also sometimes present, especially black dots randomly scattered all over the body, like a Dalmatian. Other subtle dark markings may be present, including wavy patterns on the back or sides.

Numerous combinations of these basic patterns and colors abound and continue to be developed in captivity by selective breeding. Most of the geckos that have been observed in the wild are of the duller tan to yellowish coloration with little patterning. The reason for this variance of appearance within the same species—known as polymorphism—is still poorly understood. It is not clear if different colors are found in different localities in the wild. All colors and patterns seem to effectively camouflage the geckos, allowing them to blend in with lichen- and moss-covered tree bark in their habitat.

Coloration and patterning is normally drastically different in adults and juveniles. When first hatched, the coloration of most crested geckos is usually much duller than what it will be as adults.

Patterning will usually be apparent from the beginning, but will gradually intensify as the gecko ages. Light patterning on the upper surface of the tail is usually the most contrasting feature of hatchling coloration.

In addition to the seemingly endless variety of color, each gecko is able to alter his coloration depending on his mood. The coloration and patterning doesn't change to the degree of chameleons or green anoles; it is more of a lightening or darkening of the existing colors. A gecko viewed at night can appear drastically different than in the daytime. During the daytime or in brightly lit conditions, crested gecko pigmentation will usually appear dull and less attractive than in the nighttime when they are more active. Shortly after exposure to light, the gecko will usually revert back to its daytime coloration. A stressed gecko will clearly not show his brightest colors. It is still not known if color change is used as a form of communication to other geckos, or if geckos can alter their appearance to match their background as best as they can within their limits. With some morphs, the daytime or stress colors may be more interesting than the nighttime colors. There is no correlation between coloration and a gecko's sex.

Habits and Behavior

Like all *Rhacodactylus* species, crested geckos are nocturnal. They spend the daytime in trees, curled up in the leaves. This is unlike the other species in the genus that seem to prefer to hide in tree hollows during the day. Typical activities such as feeding and breeding occur at night. Natural predators of crested geckos include the larger species of *Rhacodactylus* and may include some

Lifespan

The typical lifespan of crested geckos is not known. Based on the longevity of other similar species in captivity, it can be presumed that they can live for at least 20 years with optimal care. Given that this gecko has only been present in the hobby for about 10 years, only time will tell.

The lifespan of crested geckos in captivity is presently unknown, since the lizards have only been in the hobby since 1995

predatory birds.

It is not known if crested geckos bask in sunlight. Most nocturnally active lizards do not bask, yet its habit of living a more exposed existence in the foliage during the daytime may allow for some exposure to UV-B light from the sun, a form of ultraviolet light known to be important for calcium metabolism in many other reptiles.

Some geckos will thermoregulate (control their temperature) through behavior—they will voluntarily move to warmer or cooler spots in order to satisfy their needs. Since these geckos aren't naturally exposed to a drastic temperature change and annual temperatures remain within acceptable boundaries, there is generally no need for these geckos to bask for warmth. At the very most, they will need to leave exposed areas during warm, sunny periods to avoid getting too hot.

Males and Females

Physical differences between the sexes, a condition known as sexual dimorphism, are apparent only in mature specimens. The most noticeable feature of mature males is the presence of a large pair of bulges on the underside of the tail base. These are called the hemipenal bulges, and serve to house the pairs of retracted male copulatory organs (the hemipenes) when not mating. Well-fed hatchlings can reach sexual maturity in eight to nine months, at which point the hemipenal bulges appear very suddenly.

Another feature of adult males is a prominent row of scales with pores on the underside of the pelvic area and extending to the upper portion of the hind legs. These are called femoral pores. Females possess a similar row of scales, but the pores are not nearly as well developed. The function of these pores is not understood, but it is thought to be a means for secretion of pheromones. Pheromones are chemical signals emitted by various animals, usually as attractants for the opposite sex but also may be used for marking one's territory. Crested geckos regularly lick surfaces they are walking on and may be able to identify the presence of potential mates or competitors nearby through secretions left behind by these pores.

Many species of geckos have a pair of small bumps located on either sides of the tail base, known as the postanal tubercles. In many of these species, the male's tubercles are much larger than the female's, which make this another example of sexual dimorphism. This dimorphism is often apparent in juvenile geckos before the hemipenal bulges and femoral pores develop, and is therefore used by some breeders to sex their juveniles.

Crested geckos store calcium in sacs located in the roof of the mouth. They are the two white lumps in this gecko's mouth.

Calcium Storage

Excess calcium that is obtained from the gecko's diet is stored in the endolymphatic sacs. These sacs are easy to see on the roof of the gecko's mouth, and appear as a pair of white bumps. These reserves are utilized by the body when necessary, and are especially important in females for the process of shell development prior to laying eggs.

Crested geckos do have these tubercles, yet there is no correlation between their size and sex, and therefore is in no way a reliable means of sexing juveniles. Crested geckos can not be sexed based on their build, either. Though males of some species of geckos are more robust than females, this is not true with crested geckos.

Breeding is a seasonal event that takes place mostly during the warm, dry southern hemisphere summer. This period of time from November to April is when temperatures are averaging 80 to 85°F (26.7 to 29.4°C) and little rainfall occurs. In the winter months of May to October, rainfall is frequent and temperatures are cooler, averaging 65° to 70°F (18.3 to 21.1°C).

After mating, female *Rhacodactylus*, like many geckos, are able to store sperm for at least several months. This allows them to control the fertilization of their eggs, but the complete reasons for this adaptation are unknown. Eggs are laid in rotting logs, tree hollows, or other suitable areas that remain moist with organic debris.

Conservation

Along with much of New Caledonia's unique flora and fauna, all species of *Rhacodactylus* are considered highly threatened due to human alteration of habitats. Mining activities, agriculture, brushfires, and erosion all have a negative impact on *Rhacodactylus* habitat. In fact, very little of the original primary forest remains. Introduced animals, such as pigs, rats, cats, and dogs, all directly or indirectly affect the fragile habitat that the geckos require. As in many parts of the world, a great threat to this species is the introduced fire ant, a colony of which can easily overpower and kill an adult *Rhacodactylus*.

Legitimate importation of *Rhacodactylus* species can only be done with proper permitting procedures, and normally occurs for scientific purposes rather than for supplying the pet trade. Smuggling has clearly occurred with some species but should never be supported. It is best to never accept wild-collected geckos regardless of the source. Aside from the fact that they may be illegal, wild-collected animals are more likely to have parasites and many not adapt to captive conditions after the stress of collection and transit around the world. For all species of *Rhacodactylus*, there is enough genetic diversity in captivity to make importation of further individuals unnecessary.

Chapter 2

Crested Geckos as Pets

When deciding to purchase a crested gecko as a pet, you should first make sure you understand and can provide the requirements for proper health. You also need to understand this lizard's habits when you are determining if a crested gecko is the right lizard for you.

Crested geckos will often spend their days curled up in leaves—or in this case, a bird's nest fern.

Important Questions

Here are some things to consider when making the decision whether or not to purchase a crested gecko.

Do I Want a Lizard That Hides During the Day?

Crested geckos are nocturnal animals. Though sometimes they will be visible, they usually spend their days hiding, coming out after dark to feed and seek out mates. A hiding spot is necessary for these geckos to seclude themselves in during the day. Denying the gecko a hiding spot to make it more visible is selfishly stressing the gecko, which can lead to a decline in health. If you want to have a lizard that will be able to be seen during daylight hours, a crested gecko is not a good candidate.

Can I Provide a Proper Environment?

Many popular pet lizards require a warm spot or a basking spot in their cage so they can regulate their temperature as they need. Crested geckos on the other hand will not tolerate high temperatures and therefore shouldn't be provided with basking lights. They do best at ambient temperatures between 70° to 80°F (21.1 to 26.7°C), and will become stressed if exposed to temperatures above the mid-80s (about 29°C) range. They can, however, easily tolerate brief dips into the lower 60s range (about 16.7°C), though extended exposure to temperatures in this range or lower may cause problems.

Am I Able to Provide the Specialized Diet?

Crested geckos eat a lot of fruit and nectar in the wild, along with insects. In captivity, the fruit portion of the diet is often provided in the form of fruit baby food mixed with a powdered vitamin/mineral supplement. Pulverized or pureed fruits can also be provided. Live crickets are eagerly chased down by crested geckos, which therefore provide additional nourishment as well as exercise.

Will My Family Be Able to Safely Handle a Crested Gecko?

Crested geckos are relatively docile and not excessively fast, though they are unpredictable in their movements. Often, a crested gecko will sit calmly in your hand for several minutes, only to unexpectedly leap off. These geckos—though they appear slow moving—can move in sudden bursts of speed and quickly disappear into any available niche. Their tails break off easily, and they should never be picked up or restrained by their tails. They normally heal promptly from this injury, though infection is always possible; it is best to do everything possible to avoid such a loss. To many, the appearance of a tailless crested gecko is less desirable than one with a full tail. Therefore, the value of the gecko decreases once the tail is lost, as it does not regenerate like it does in some other lizard species.

Children should always be supervised when allowed to handle pet crested geckos. Though crested geckos can be handled safely after learning how the animal behaves, this species is not necessarily as tolerant and sturdy as some of the other more commonly available species, such as leopard geckos and bearded dragons. They rarely bite (and are unlikely to break the skin if they do), but an annoyed gecko is more likely to become stressed, which can lead to a decline in health. It is best to keep crested geckos as animals to observe, not to take out and handle. They are not animals to show off or take out to play with. Some feel that their gecko must "like them" or "likes being held" because it doesn't run away when being held. This is far from the case, as they do not bond with their owners like dogs and cats. Just because a gecko doesn't show discomfort doesn't mean he isn't greatly affected by a stressful situation such as handling.

Salmonella Risks

As with all reptiles, there is the possibility of contracting a *Salmonella* bacterial infection (salmonellosis) from crested geckos. This can result in severe gastric distress and diarrhea and—in severe cases—can be fatal. Anyone who handles reptiles should always thoroughly wash their hands afterwards. Although there is some risk of getting salmonellosis from you gecko and you should take precautions against contracting it, remember to put the risk in perspective. There is probably more risk of getting salmonellosis from eating undercooked chicken and eggs as there is from handling your gecko.

Can It Live With My Other Pet Lizard?

It is best to not mix different species of reptiles. This is stressful to the inhabitants, competition for food is likely, and one may eat or injure the other. Supplying the drastically different needs for both lizards will normally be impossible in the same cage. If the desire to combine species comes down to the simple fact that you don't want to purchase (or don't have space for) another cage, it is highly recommended that you reconsider purchasing another reptile.

Purchasing a Crested Gecko

Before purchasing any reptile, you should make sure to have a cage with all the necessary furnishings set up in advance. Fortunately, most supplies can be purchased at any pet store that offers reptiles. It is advisable to have a source of properly sized crickets secured in advance as well. If your local pet store or fishing bait shop doesn't carry the proper sized crickets, they may be able to put a special order in for you. If crickets are not available in your area, you may need to have them shipped to you. Once you have set up your cage and have a reliable source of food items, you can now begin looking for your new pet.

When seeking your first crested gecko, try to shop around if possible. Quality of health varies depending on the supplier and the gecko's living conditions. If you buy from a pet shop, check to see that the staff has the proper knowledge to care for their reptiles, especially with regards to vitamin supplementation and diet. Sadly, despite the rising popularity of pet reptiles, many pet store employees still don't always know the specialized requirements of all their different types of animals. A gecko that has not been cared for properly will be in a state of stress, which can continue to worsen and create other health problems even after he is finally receiving proper care in your home. Rescuing an improperly cared for reptile from a pet store and rehabilitating it is rewarding, but unfortunately not something everyone can do without knowledge of diagnosing and treating reptilian health problems.

Virtually all of the crested geckos on the market are captive bred, so they are normally healthy and free of parasites.

Of course there are reputable pet shops with excellent reptile products and knowledge, and, of course, these are favorable sources for quality animals. Aside from pet stores, there are many commercial and private reptile breeders that provide quality animals. Some specialize in crested geckos, and it is from these breeders that one can choose from a wider variety of colors and ages of crested geckos. Some breeders will be selling crested geckos fresh out of the egg to avoid having to take care of them, while other breeders prefer to head-start their hatchlings, keeping them for several weeks before offering them for sale. This ensures that their animals are healthy and feeding, which is preferable to purchasing a freshly hatched crested gecko.

Another source for healthy crested geckos is one of the many reptile shows held at least annually in larger cities. Often, breeders will have a wide selection to choose from, and will usually be very willing to share helpful advice. It is a convenient way to shop around with various vendors at the same time.

Still another source is the Internet, where many breeders have websites offering their current inventory, and some even have pictures of individual geckos allowing the buyer to choose the one he likes. There are many websites created by serious crested gecko hobbyists as

Selecting a Healthy Gecko

When choosing your pet, there are several things you should look for to make sure you pick a healthy gecko. It may be difficult to assess a crested gecko's health by just looking in its enclosure, so ask to hold the gecko for closer inspection. Familiarize yourself with the appearance of a healthy crested gecko of proper body weight and settle for no less.

This list will help you find a healthy gecko.

- Make sure the crested gecko has acceptable body weight. The first clear sign that a crested gecko is losing weight is protruding hip bones, even though the rest of the body may seem bulky.
- Check to make sure there are no external blemishes such as bite marks, skin tears, sores, rashes, etc.
- The eyes should be clear and not sunken into the head. Pupils should appear as thin slits under normal room lighting conditions. If the pupils are widely dilated under typical lighting, the gecko may have health issues.
- Check the ears, nostrils, and vent to make sure they are clean and free of obstructions. Make sure there are no pieces of shed skin retained anywhere on the body.
- Look closely for the presence of mites on the skin, especially in tight places like the armpits.
- Check for kinks in the spine, pelvis, and tail bones. Whether the gecko has a tail or not is a matter of personal preference, but if it is missing a tail make sure the stump is completely healed over.
- When holding the gecko, gently run your fingers along the underside of the abdomen. If any hard masses are felt, this could indicate a possible impaction or retained egg.
- Gently encourage the gecko to climb up your arm. If it has difficulty climbing or adhering to a surface, this may indicate the gecko has a serious problem.

Along with the gecko itself, inspect the gecko's caging and care. Check to see that the gecko's feces are healthy and well formed—not liquefied. Make sure the seller has been providing the basic needs for the gecko. Ask what the geckos are eating, and what supplementation they receive. If the gecko you are interested in is being kept with other geckos, check to see if they appear healthy as well.

If there is any question about the health of the gecko, it is best to avoid purchasing it altogether. Do not purchase from someone who is not taking care of their animals properly. If a gecko has been stressed due to a vendor's improper care, the additional stress of transporting the gecko home and setting it up in a new environment may be too much for the gecko to handle.

well, and searching these sites will often provide good leads on reputable online sources for quality animals.

If you order your crested geckos from a distant source, make sure the seller is knowledgeable with shipping live reptiles properly. Shipping during the winter and summer months is tricky, as the package containing the reptiles may be exposed to a variety of temperature extremes that can be fatal. Heat packs and cold packs are used by some breeders during these times of the year, but even these can cause harm if not used properly. Crested geckos are normally shipped in plastic deli cups with ventilation holes punched in the sides, and with a slightly damp paper towel on the bottom of the cup. These are packed in cardboard boxes insulated with foam inserts. Reptiles should only be shipped for overnight delivery, and should never be in transit for longer than 24 hours.

Acclimation

When bringing home a newly purchased crested gecko, it is best to avoid handling it for several days. This prevents the gecko from having to undergo additional stress, and it allows the gecko to get used to his new environment. Make sure to provide hiding places to make him feel more secure and avoid any contact for a day or two.

Breeders will have a selection of colorful cresteds for sale, perhaps including a few oddly color individuals like this one.

If the gecko was shipped to you, he has just gone through a very stressful experience during shipping. After a long time in transit, the gecko will be thirsty. After unpacking, it is important to mist the gecko's new cage, allowing water droplets to form on the sides of the cage and furnishings for the gecko to lick up. A water bowl should be available as well, but the new arrival will likely prefer to lick up the water droplets. Though it may eat shortly after arrival, don't worry if the gecko refuses food for a day or two.

Chapter 3

Housing

Crested geckos are not very demanding when it comes to proper caging. Caging may be as simple as a lidded plastic sweater storage container with drilled ventilation holes, or it may be an elaborate naturalistic vivarium with living plants and a waterfall. Regardless of the type you decide on, it is important to make sure the caging of your choice is escape-proof, will provide adequate ventilation, and maintains proper humidity and temperature. It should also provide a reasonable amount of room and hiding spaces and allow for easy access for feeding and cleaning.

Cage types

A common choice for a crested gecko enclosure is a standard glass aquarium. A 10-gallon (38 l) aquarium will provide enough room for one adult crested gecko; a pair should be kept in at least a 15-gallon aquarium (58 l), and a trio in at least a 20-gallon (76 l) aquarium. The more geckos housed together, the more room you should provide. A variety of styles of lids are made for aquariums, and those with small built-in doors will minimize the possibility of escape when offering food. Make sure the lid is tight-fitting. Ventilation is important, and therefore your choice of lids should factor this in as well. Avoid acrylic aquariums, as they tend to get scratched during cleaning, making for an unappealing display.

Separate the Boys

As long as you have enough space in the enclosure, you should have no problem housing a small group of crested geckos together. However, if more than one of those geckos is a male, there will be problems. When the males become mature, they will start fighting. You may not see them skirmish, but you will see the bite wounds and missing tails. To avoid this, house only one male per enclosure.

Another inexpensive caging option is a transparent plastic storage box, which is sometimes referred to as a sweater box—though there are many different styles and sizes. Try to find a brand that has a secure-fitting lid. Ventilation holes will need to be drilled in the sides of the cage. You can also use a soldering iron to make the holes quickly, but remember to do so in a well-ventilated area. There are now suppliers of these boxes who cater to the reptile hobby and sell boxes that come with pre-drilled air holes. Some breeders construct racks that hold several of these plastic storage boxes that slide in and out like drawers. In some models, the boxes don't have lids, so the racks need to be constructed out of a non-porous material, such as melamine, to allow for easy cleaning.

A preferable option for housing multiple crested geckos together is a screen cage. Some brands have flexible netting that slides over a plastic framework, with doors secured by zippers on both ends. These are made specifically for reptiles and are available at many pet stores and online. Similar cages can be constructed out of six metal frames of aluminum window screen secured together, with hinged and latching doors on one or two ends. These cages don't retain as much humidity as the solid-walled options and, therefore, need to be misted more regularly in drier environments.

Custom-made wooden cages with glass panels are not recommended. Even when the wood is sealed with polyurethane, the humid environment that crested geckos require will still warp the wood and distort the cage. Since crested geckos often defecate on the walls of the cage, regular scrubbing of the polyurethane-coated wood may scratch the surface or wear down to unsealed wood.

Temperature

Crested geckos do best when kept at an ambient temperature

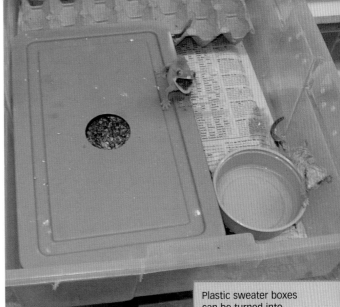

Plastic sweater boxes can be turned into suitable gecko housing and are especially useful if you have a large colony.

between 72° and 80°F (22.2 and 26.7°C). Temperatures higher than the mid-80s will stress the animals. Crested geckos can easily tolerate brief temperature drops in the lower 60s range (about 16.7°C), though they should not be kept at these temperatures for very long. Crested geckos will thrive in a room heated in the winter and air conditioned in the summer, and usually will not require any additional heating source.

Since they are nocturnal and don't bask or otherwise require a warm spot, a heat source is generally not a requirement if the ambient room temperature is kept above 70°F (21.1°C). If a heat source is required during cooler months, your cage size

A 10-gallon (38 l) aquarium turned on its end can make a nice captive habitat for a crested gecko or two.

No Hot Rocks

Do not use a hot rock—electrically heated fake stones—under any circumstance for crested geckos or any type of reptile, as these have been responsible for numerous burns. Additionally, they sometimes develop shorts that will shock your pet. There are much safer methods to provide heat to your reptiles.

and configuration will dictate the type of heat source you should use. For smaller aquariums up to about 20 gallons (76 l), an incandescent bulb or a ceramic heater that screws into an incandescent fixture would be preferable, as it creates radiant heat that warms the entire enclosure.

With crested geckos, it would be ineffective to use an undertank reptile heat pad or a strip of heat tape, since the heat is not as easily dispersed throughout the tank from these sources. Though heat pads and heat strips will create warm spots, crested geckos will not necessarily seek out these places when temperatures drop and may choose to hide in their preferred niche rather than go find a warmer spot.

When using incandescent bulbs as heat sources, make sure there are adequate dark hiding areas, as the geckos will shun the light. It is important to experiment with different wattages of bulbs to determine which will provide the optimum temperature in the cages. Monitor this very closely to avoid getting the geckos too hot, and use a reliable thermometer—digital ones sold at electronic stores are the most accurate type.

The easiest and safest way to heat any crested gecko enclosure is to simply heat the room itself. Inexpensive portable heaters can do the job just fine, as long as room conditions are monitored regularly.

Conversely, cooling will be required in areas that experience hot summers. Air conditioning the room is the only reliable way to cool a crested gecko cage. If you are using lights over your crested gecko cage, remember during warmer months that this will increase the temperature in the cage. Again, a thermometer should be a permanent part of every crested gecko cage.

Humidity

Humidity is a requirement that must not be overlooked. If the relative humidity is not adequate, the geckos may experience shedding problems, which could lead to severe problems and even death. Dehydration can also result from low levels of humidity. Hatchlings and juvenile crested geckos are particularly dependant on high levels of humidity to help with their frequent shedding. Purchasing a hygrometer, a device that measures relative humidity, is recommended, especially in exceptionally dry regions. The relative humidity should be between 70 to 80 percent. If it is falling below this level, frequently, misting the sides of the cage with a spray bottle is recommended.

Humidity will be less of a problem when live plants are used, assuming the plants are watered regularly. Certain substrates, such as cypress mulch, will also retain moisture, and therefore, help maintain humidity levels.

In extremely dry regions, a humidifier may be a wise investment. With this equipment, the room can be kept at the proper humidity, reducing the need to regularly mist the enclosure.

Light

A crested gecko's need for natural sunlight is poorly understood. Though they are nocturnal, they spend the day hiding in leaves on the outer branches of trees in the wild. Under these circumstances, we might assume they get at least some exposure to natural light. The B wavelength of ultraviolet light (UV-B) from natural sunlight is necessary for proper nutrition of some other reptiles that are active during the daytime. It is not known if crested geckos will benefit from exposure to natural sunlight, or the artificial reptile lights that emit the UV-B wavelength. Since captive crested geckos often prefer to retire during the day under newspaper substrate or a dark

Crested geckos require humidity levels of 70 to 80 percent for normal skin shedding and general good health.

recess, they don't seem to appreciate being exposed to excessive amounts of light. Plenty of breeders have been successful without using any type of lighting on their cages.

If lighting is desired or necessary for plants, make sure to provide enough hiding places or plant cover so your gecko can feel secure. For larger vivariums, special fluorescent bulbs with high output may be necessary for some types of plants. These bulbs don't work in typical light fixtures made for lower wattage bulbs, and require the correct type of ballast to operate them. Even though there may appear to be enough light, conditions in a vivarium are not identical to being exposed to the sunlight. Plants will be deformed and stretching towards the light if it is not bright enough, creating an unappealing display. Avoid metal halide or other conventional lights as they emit extraordinary amounts of heat, which will be disliked by the crested geckos.

No Sunlight

Avoid placing cages near a window or otherwise in direct sunlight. The sun shining through a window on a cage even for a short period of time can raise the temperature to harmful levels. Sunlight can only be used in larger greenhouses and conservatories in which the temperature is controlled.

Substrate

There are many choices for cage substrate. Some of these are a matter of personal preference, while others may be more difficult to clean than others. A simple substrate that works well is regular newspaper. When it becomes soiled, simply discard it and replace it with some new sheets.

Some keepers find newspaper unappealing in display cages. They may opt for other more natural-looking substrates. Some of these include cypress mulch, peat moss, sphagnum moss, dried leaves, and soil. These substrates will hold moisture to varying degrees, but should not be allowed to stay wet. When cleaning, these substrates can be spot-cleaned by simply scooping out the feces. These substrates should be completely replaced every several months or less depending on the number of geckos in the enclosure.

Several companies are manufacturing another type of substrate that is made from shredded recycled paper. It is absorbent, can be easily spot-cleaned, and the geckos can readily burrow in it. It seems to hold up to humid environments without growing mold but may become messy and need regular changing if misted frequently.

Newspaper is a safe and inexpensive substrate for a *Rhacodactylus* enclosure.

Avoid granular substrates, like aquarium gravel, that can accidentally be ingested during feeding and lead to a gut impaction, a possibly fatal condition. Be sure to use only soil that you are sure is clean and free of fertilizers, pesticides, and other contaminants that may harm your geckos. Also avoid sand, calcium carbonate, or similar fine-particulate substrates. These are often dusty, and any dust that gets in the lamellae will impede the gecko's ability to climb up surfaces.

Hiding Areas

Since crested geckos are nocturnal, hiding places are necessary for daytime security. This is especially true if a light is used over the cage, as in a planted tank, but even when a light is not used, hiding places will be appreciated.

Various items can serve as a hiding place. A box with an entrance hole will work, as will things like sections of PVC pipe and paper towel roll cores. When newspaper is used as a substrate, crested geckos will often prefer to hide underneath it, ignoring other intended hiding spots.

For a more natural look, cork bark is an excellent choice. Cork is harvested mostly in Spain and Portugal, where the thick outer layer of bark is cut off the tree, either in curved slabs, or tubular hollow branch sections. The tree is not harmed in the process, as another layer of bark will eventually regenerate for a future harvest. Various sizes of cork slabs and rounds are often

Include climbing surfaces, such as tree branches and live plants, in your crested gecko enclosure.

sold specifically for reptile hiding spots at pet shops. Cork is also very resistant to rot, and works well in a planted vivarium. Aside from providing security to the crested geckos, you can mount orchids, bromeliads, or other epiphytic plants to the cork for an additional touch of naturalism.

If you have a lushly planted vivarium, there will likely be plenty of hiding spots available. Try to use some plants with large, densely packed foliage, and be thinking of hiding places when constructing the vivarium.

Never deny a crested gecko its hiding spots so it can be visible all the time. A gecko in this situation is not happy, and this unnecessary stress can lead to serious health problems.

The Vivarium

For the ambitious, a planted vivarium is a very appealing option for housing crested geckos. An easily maintained vivarium can contain potted plants for the geckos to hide in and climb on, while the most complex of vivariums may appear like a slice of the crested gecko's natural habitat, complete with a variety of exotic tropical plants, rockwork, and driftwood artistically arranged and covered with living moss, a wet section complete with fish, and even a small waterfall.

When constructing a basic vivarium, try to keep it simple enough to allow for easy cleaning. A few easy-to-care-for potted houseplants, such as the common variegated pothos, *Epipremnum aureum*, can be positioned toward the back of the cage, allowing the vines to hang down and conceal the pot. Driftwood or cork bark can also be used to conceal the pot. A layer of dried leaves, cypress mulch, or commercially available substrates derived from ground coconut shells and other natural materials can be used to make a natural looking substrate. Rocks should be avoided as they can shift and crush a gecko hiding nearby. Daily misting will be beneficial to both the plants and the geckos, which will eagerly lap up the droplets off the leaves. When the plant's leaves get soiled from the geckos defecating on them, the potted plant can be removed and sprayed off with a hose.

Cage Mates

All species of *Rhacodactylus* do best with members of the same species that are of similar size and health. Some beginners want to mix a variety of reptiles in the same cage, usually due to a desire for a new species to add to their collection coupled with a reluctance to purchase a new cage and accompanying supplies. It is best to avoid mixing other species of lizards or other animals in the same cage. *Rhacodactylus* may decide to eat any living thing small enough to swallow, or the cage mate may decide to eat the *Rhacodactylus*. The interactions of various species may be stressful on some or all inhabitants and competition for food is likely to occur, especially if diurnal animals are mixed with nocturnal species. Though the thought of a naturalistic exhibit featuring several species of lizards, frogs, insects, or other animals may be very tempting, it is best left to zoos and museums to attempt to create on a larger scale. It can be done successfully with the right mixture of species, but *Rhacodactylus* generally can't be kept with the commonly kept types of lizards such as leopard geckos, fat-tail geckos, bearded dragons, etc.

Aside from plants, natural decorative materials such as driftwood, cork bark panels or round sections, or rocks are strategically placed to form the non-living landscape that gives your vivarium a more realistic look. Make sure any driftwood used is of a type that is resistant to rot. Cypress and buttonwood are good choices. Though it is also very resistant to rot, avoid cedar because the phenols contained in the wood are harmful to reptiles. When building the foundation, allow niches for the placement of plants, and always make sure these items are secured with suitable adhesives or fasteners to avoid collapses that could result in crushed geckos.

Lighting

In order to keep the plants healthy, you will need to supply light. A fluorescent light fixture can be purchased from a pet store and used with great results. Since crested geckos are nocturnal, they will normally be hiding when the fluorescent lights are on. Therefore, make sure there are adequate places for them to conceal themselves. Since they don't bask and UV light probably isn't important to crested geckos, expensive "reptile bulbs" are not necessary, and standard plant grow-lights available at hardware stores will work great. Do not use

Live moss, available at specialty nurseries and online suppliers, makes an appealing substrate in a crested gecko vivarium.

incandescent lights, as they emit too much heat and are not of a spectrum that plants generally prefer.

Water

Water features in a vivarium will also require research and planning in order to be successful. Keep in mind that feces will end up in the water, as well as any crickets not eaten immediately. Together, they will quickly pollute the water, creating unhealthy conditions. These pleasing additions to a vivarium are best used in only the larger vivariums, and are still best left to the experts.

Other Considerations

If you wish to set up a more complex naturalistic vivarium, additional research and planning will be necessary. Conditions in an improperly set-up vivarium will soon deteriorate to the point where all but the hardiest plants will die, wet areas will become foul, and conditions will be unsuitable for the geckos. In order to keep optimum conditions, you must provide good air circulation, good substrate drainage, regular misting, and decent light. If these parameters are not met, the plant and animal occupants will not flourish. A damp substrate that lacks drainage will become a haven for anaerobic bacterial growth, which will create conditions unsuitable for plants and animals and emit a foul smell. Various methods of creating the proper vivarium conditions can be researched on the Internet.

Drainage Layer

Having a drainage layer in a naturalistic setup will help keep conditions from becoming swampy and stagnant. The drainage layer is a foundation of gravel or perlite that goes under the soil or substrate. This layer should be at least two inches deep to allow excess water to sink into it without making the substrate soggy.

For that extra touch of authenticity, you can include native New Caledonian plants in your vivarium. From left to right: bird's nest fern, a native orchid (*Bulbophyllum* sp.), and split-leafed *Epipremnum pinnatum*.

Larger displays can be created that incorporate small trees. These setups can take the form of large or outdoor cages to small conservatories or greenhouses. Since wild crested geckos prefer to live in the leaves and twigs on the outer parts of branches, they will have the opportunity to behave in a more natural manner in this setup. Good choices for small trees would be various types of *Ficus* sp. that are commonly sold for interior decorating. In the larger greenhouses and conservatories, other larger tropical trees and shrubs, including various palms, cycads, bananas, heliconias, etc. can be used. Keep in mind that your geckos will normally be difficult to locate in these large enclosures, and finding eggs may be nearly impossible. Using this method will require knowledge of greenhouse construction, heating, cooling, and plant care. If conditions are right, hatchlings may be able to grow to adulthood in large, lushly planted conservatories without any human intervention other than providing proper temperatures and making sure food is available.

Maintenance

A regular cage maintenance schedule should be followed to keep the habitat clean. With arboreal geckos, feces often get deposited on the sides of the cage, obstructing the view in glass aquariums and making the cage look dirty quickly. The geckos will walk through the

Plants From the Homeland

Some ambitious hobbyists may prefer to set up a cage containing native New Caledonian plant species, creating a slice of the crested gecko's habitat. There are some tropical houseplants, both rarely and commonly available at garden centers or specialty nurseries, that occur naturally in the crested gecko's habitat. Here are a few native ferns that are regularly available in larger garden centers and nurseries:

• Bird's nest fern, *Asplenium nidum*

• Staghorn fern, *Platycerium bifurcatum*

• Dwarf tree fern, *Blechnum gibbum*

Other New Caledonian plant species are typically grown by rare plant collectors and specialty nurseries. You can search through literature or the Internet to learn about other native species, and then search online nursery catalogs for those that interest you. Some other native plant species that can be tracked down are the semi-succulent, vining *Hoya limoniaca* and the climbing *Epipremnum pinnatum*, with its shiny emerald-green split leaves. A few types of orchids live in New Caledonia, including several species of *Bulbophyllum*. Some of these may be found at nurseries that specialize in rare orchid species. Some of these rare species of plants may be difficult to care for, so you should research the requirements of the plants you are interested in before you buy them.

fruit mixture they are fed, often tracking it all over the cage. These conditions—combined with humidity—lead to a very unsanitary environment, which will negatively affect your gecko's health.

The walls of the cage should be cleaned at least weekly. How often this is done will depend on the number of geckos within the enclosure. Scrubbing with a damp towel will work well. Do not use cleaning chemicals inside the cage with the animals.

The floor of the cage should be cleaned regularly as well. If you are using newspaper, it should be replaced on a weekly basis or as necessary. Since the geckos will often hide under the paper, the bottom of the cage should be scrubbed with a damp cloth at this time if necessary. If live potted plants are used, they should be removed and any fecal matter gently washed off. Artificial plants can be cleaned as well.

In a naturalistic vivarium, maintenance will be more complicated. You will still need to be cleaning the glass sides whenever necessary. A natural vivarium should never be overpopulated, and there should be a balance between the number of plants and geckos. This way, the enclosed environment will be able to "consume" the wastes produced from the geckos through the action of beneficial bacteria in the substrate and absorption by the plants. If this natural decomposition of wastes is not happening at an acceptable rate—feces are accumulating and the vivarium emits a foul odor—you are probably overcrowding the geckos. The best solution would be to set up another enclosure and move a few individuals into the new cage.

Cage Maintenance Schedule

Follow this schedule to maintain clean and healthy living conditions for your geckos. Be aware that these are general guidelines, and certain tasks will need to be done more frequently in cages that house large groups of geckos.

Every Day:

- Check to see that the water bowl is clean. Give clean water if necessary.
- Check temperatures in the cage and adjust heating or cooling devices when necessary.
- Remove uneaten fruit puree and any dead feeder insects from the previous day's feeding.
- Mist walls of cage and plants with a spray bottle.
- If breeding animals are present, check nesting sites for eggs, and make sure laying medium is clean and properly moistened.

Every Week:

- Clean feces from walls of cage.
- Change newspaper or manually remove (spot clean) feces from substrate
- Clean cage accessories (artificial or real plants, branches, nesting/hide boxes, etc.)
- Water any live plants.
- Sanitize water bowl.

Every Month:

- Completely break down the cage and sanitize it and furnishings with 10 percent bleach solution. Add new substrate to clean cage. This is not necessary if you have a vivarium with potting soil and live plants.

Chapter 4

Feeding and Nutrition

The condition an animal is exposed to in captivity is far removed from what it experiences in its natural habitat. A captive animal's diet is often inferior to the foods and nutrients it consumes in the wild. There is much to be learned about a reptile's natural diet in order to provide a similar diet for our animals. As with all aspects of reptile keeping, we are limited to the experiences of those who have failed or succeeded through experimentation with various methods. The development of a balanced captive diet through understanding the animal's wild diet is one of the most important necessities determining the success and future of any animal that is available only through captive breeding.

Crested geckos and the other *Rhacodactylus* are omnivores, eating a mix of insects and fruit.

Though crested geckos are successfully kept and bred in large numbers by many individuals, we can not say that a balanced captive diet has been developed just yet. Breeders regularly experience several health problems in their animals that may be attributed to nutritional imbalances. Until more research is done, only those methods that have clearly been the most successful can be recommended.

Crested geckos and other *Rhacodactylus* are omnivores, meaning they eat both plant and animal material. In the wild, these geckos consume a variety of insects and small vertebrates. They may even cannibalize juveniles of their own kind. Their vegetarian preferences include nectar and pollen from flowers, and they will consume whole berry-like fruits. They are not known to eat any leafy material or other vegetables typically preferred by other herbivorous lizards, such as iguanas and bearded dragons.

Insect Foods

Crickets and other fast-moving insects are eagerly hunted and eaten by all individuals. Crested geckos seem to love to chase after crickets, which also may provide important exercise. The common domestic or brown cricket, *Acheta domestica*, is one of the most easily obtainable feeder insects and is highly recommended. Most pet stores that specialize in reptiles will carry them in several sizes, and fishing bait stores in certain areas will also carry them. If unavailable in your area, there are many cricket farms that advertise in reptile magazines or on the Internet that can ship crickets through the mail to your door.

Cricket Care

Crickets should be kept in a container large enough to prevent overcrowding. Cardboard egg crate material, often included in cricket shipments, is recommended to use in the cricket container to provide additional surface area. Paper towel and toilet paper rolls can also be used. Sides of the container should be tall, at least 24 inches (61 cm) high to prevent the crickets from jumping out. The walls of the container should be smooth to prevent crickets from climbing out. If the container is of a material that the crickets can climb, a secure screen lid must be used.

Crickets at pet shops often live on nothing more than potatoes. A cricket under these conditions provides little in the way of useable nutrition for your geckos. In order to be nutritionally valuable, crickets must be fed a varied diet of fruits and vegetables. A mixture of apples, citrus fruits, leafy greens, squash, etc. should be available at all times to your crickets. The crickets will ingest these foods (called gut-loading), and your geckos will in turn obtain these nutrients from your crickets. Make sure to always wash any fruit or vegetables well to avoid possible poisoning from pesticide residues. Cricket gut-loading feed is commercially available in dry granular form, but should not be viewed as a replacement for fruits and vegetables, which provide necessary moisture to the crickets.

Just because a cricket is gut-loaded doesn't mean it is nutritionally adequate. Some supplementation with vitamins and minerals is also required to round out your gecko's diet. See the section on supplements later in this chapter for details.

Crickets for hatchling geckos, like this baby gargoyle gecko, must be small—no bigger than the length of the gecko's head.

When Crickets Attack

Loose crickets running around in your gecko's cage are more than a nuisance; they can actually be dangerous. Hungry crickets will eat just about anything. This can include the plants in the cage or, worse, your gecko. Crickets have been known to cause serious damage to the eyes and toes of lizards and even kill hatchlings and slow-moving species. So, be careful not to provide too many crickets, and remove any excess you may see.

Feeding Crickets to Crested Geckos

Crickets come in a variety of sizes, and you will need to purchase several sizes if you are raising your own hatchlings along with feeding the parents. When determining the proper size of cricket to feed, look at the length of the gecko's head. Crested geckos can easily eat crickets that are equal in length to their head. Fresh hatchlings will easily be able to consume quarter-inch crickets and transition to half-inch crickets several months later. A few months later, they will feed on adult crickets and continue to do so for the remainder of their growth. If you are not sure, it is better to offer crickets on the smaller side, but don't go to the extent of offering an adult gecko something as small as quarter-inch crickets, as it will have a difficult time catching enough to make a good meal.

Avoid adding too many crickets to the cage. A new hatchling will eat two to three quarter-inch crickets each feeding, while an adult may eat seven or eight adult crickets at a time. You will know when you are feeding too many, as the excess adult crickets will be chirping at night while you are trying to sleep. Excess crickets are bothersome to reptiles and can even cause stress if the gecko can not escape from them. Without food, these leftover insects will end up dying and rotting if not removed soon.

Crickets running loose in the cage may end up in the water bowl, where they will drown and putrefy if they can't get out. Some people put small inert objects in the water bowl for the cricket to climb up on and jump out. A small clean pebble that sticks up above the water surface works well for this purpose. It is not perfectly effective, but will minimize the need to change the water bowl.

Freeze dried crickets are becoming more available in some pet stores. This product is for those who don't want to deal with live crickets chirping all night and escaping in the house. Crested geckos don't seem interested in eating dried crickets, though at least one company is making a vibrating plate that gives life to dried crickets for those reptiles that prefer to hunt down moving prey. This may or may not work, depending on your gecko.

Catching Gecko Food

Some keepers prefer to collect their own insects to feed to their reptiles. This is risky, especially in areas sprayed for mosquitoes or other pests. Collecting can be done by sweeping nets through low vegetation. It is not advisable to feed collected insects, as some insects may cause injury to your geckos through bites or toxins, and others, such as hard-shelled beetles, may cause intestinal impactions.

Mealworms and Other Prey

Mealworms, wax worms and other similar types of insect larvae are often refused, probably because they are slow moving. Some geckos will eat them but not with the same ferocity with which they consume crickets. Some species of roaches are becoming available as feeder insects from a few sources, and they would probably be an excellent alternative food item for *Rhacodactylus* species. Pinky mice have also been offered but with little success.

Fruit and Processed Foods

Many keepers prefer to satisfy a crested gecko's need for sweet fruits and nectar with a fruit baby food mix. Jars of baby food in a variety of flavors are inexpensive and readily available everywhere. Banana, peach, guava, and papaya baby food seem to be liked by most geckos. Some will have dislikes, while others will eat any flavor put in front of them. Therefore, experimentation may be necessary to see what certain geckos prefer. Meat baby food mixed with the fruit flavors will add necessary protein to the diet, with turkey or chicken being used most often by breeders. Crested geckos don't seem to prefer the meat baby food, so no more than one-quarter of the mixture should consist of meat flavors. Vitamin supplementation should be mixed in as well.

Supplemented baby food mixture should be offered in a small plate or dish. Lids to empty baby food jars work well and are handy for this purpose. Place the dish with baby food in a central location where it won't be easily tipped over, or place it near your gecko's favorite hiding place. Often the geckos will sense the fresh baby food shortly after it is put into the

Variety Is Best

A few breeders claim to exclusively feed supplemented baby food to their geckos, and never offer crickets. It is recommended to offer as varied of a diet as possible, which includes both crickets and baby food. Aside from the additional protein, hunting crickets is generally the only exercise geckos experience in captivity, and the indigestible exoskeletons add necessary roughage to the diet.

Crested geckos relish fruit baby foods, and it is easy to mix in supplements.

cage and will soon come out and begin lapping it up. Other individuals may be shy and will only eat at night when the lights are out. Learn your animal's habits and adjust your feeding schedule appropriately.

Never let uneaten baby food mixture sit for longer than 12 hours, as it will quickly become rancid and will lead to unsanitary conditions. Always remove the dish that the baby food was offered on after your geckos are finished eating. Learn how much your geckos will eat in one sitting, and do not offer more than they will eat. Be careful with offering large portions to group cages, especially with hatchlings. Hatchlings can get mired down in the sticky mixture, and could suffocate should they happen to jump in it or try to walk through it.

If they don't get stuck, excessive amounts of baby food on their feet could interfere with their ability to climb. Unfortunately, crested geckos will often walk through the baby food, tracking it all over the cage, which can lead to moldy conditions if not cleaned up promptly.

An alternative to baby food is fruit puree. Various fruits, along with vitamin supplementation, can be blended in a food processor and offered to your geckos in the same manner as mentioned for baby food. Soft fruits, like bananas, can be easily mashed up and presented as well.

Commercially Prepared Diets

At least one company is offering a powdered diet specifically formulated for feeding crested geckos. The powder is mixed with a small amount of water

For the Birds (and Geckos)

Another prepared-food option used by a few breeders is a powdered food mix intended for use with lories and lorikeets, parrot-type birds that feed on fruit and nectar. The powdered lory food is mixed with a certain amount of water (follow the directions on the package) to form a semi-liquid consistency. Lory food is available at some pets stores and most bird specialty shops.

and offered on a plate like baby food. The company claims this is a nutritionally complete diet, eliminating the need to offer crickets, making it desirable to those who would prefer to not deal with crickets. Though some breeders use it exclusively, others have poor success with it. Some geckos seem to eat it with no problems, while others will turn their nose up at it. A gecko with a taste for baby food may be reluctant to make the transition to this diet without mixing some baby food with it, and then gradually reducing the amount of baby food. Better success is had with starting out feeding the diet to hatchlings from day one. There will still be some individuals that will refuse it, in which case you will need to watch closely and be prepared with crickets and baby food so they don't starve.

Supplementation

Providing all the necessary vitamins and minerals is one of the most important aspects to keeping reptiles in captivity as well as the most confusing and widely debated. A gecko in the wild obtains everything he needs from his unique native diet. He also may pick up various minerals and trace elements intentionally at naturally occurring deposits, or inadvertently when feeding or licking up water droplets off of various surfaces. Native insects naturally gut-loaded on New Caledonian vegetation may have drastically different nutritional components than "properly" gut-loaded, captive-raised crickets.

Crested geckos in captivity must have their food regularly supplemented with a proper combination of vitamins and minerals. Nutritional problems will result from either not enough or too much vitamins or minerals, and certain combinations can cause problems as well. Unfortunately, the required amounts of vitamins, minerals, and trace elements are poorly understood. Preferred supplementation methods vary among breeders and are solely based on the degree of success resulting from experimentation.

Most breeders prefer to use powdered supplements. Some brands of powdered

The Importance of Supplements

The importance of supplementing your gecko's food with a multivitamin power and calcium with vitimin D$_3$ must not be overlooked. Simply put, the health of a gecko offered exclusively a diet of unsupplemented insects and fruit puree will deteriorate to the point that it will need to be euthanized. Often, clear symptoms of an inadequate diet are only apparent when the problem is in advanced (and untreatable) stages. It is up to you to make sure your pet's health never declines to this point in the first place.

supplements are ground more finely than others. When dusting crickets, the finer powder will adhere better to insects than the more coarse powder. A few breeders use liquid bird vitamins mixed in pureed diets.

These nutritional enhancements are available in the form of calcium supplements, multivitamin supplements, and supplements containing both calcium and multivitamins. It is not recommended to assume one brand is complete enough for your geckos. Combinations of calcium supplementation and multivitamin supplements should be used. Finding the proper balance of calcium and multivitamins will depend on the brand(s) used.

Calcium

Calcium is extremely important to growing juveniles, especially for skeletal development. It is also important for breeding females, as calcium reserves are quickly depleted in the process of eggshell formation. Vitamin D_3 is necessary for the utilization of calcium, and therefore needs to be a component of a calcium supplemental regime. The intake of vitamin D_3 needs to be regulated, though. Lack of enough D_3 will obviously hinder the metabolism of calcium. On the other hand, too much vitamin D_3 will allow for excessive absorption of calcium, which can also cause severe problems. It is best to read the labels of the brands of supplements available, and when mixing calcium supplements with multivitamin supplements, make sure only one of the two types contains vitamin D_3 to avoid overdosing.

Some reptiles that bask in the daylight, such as green iguanas, require exposure to ultraviolet-B light which is critical for the synthesis of vitamin D_3. Though this is obtained from sunlight in the wild, special

Add calcium and a multivitamin/multimineral supplement to your crested's diet to ensure good health.

Separate the Calcium

Calcium supplements are usually sold separate from multivitamin supplements for a good reason. If they were kept mixed together for any substantial length of time, some of the nutrients would deteriorate when in contact with another. Mix the two types of supplementation together only when feeding not when storing.

reptile lights that emit UV-B are available for this purpose. It is so far unknown if UV-B light is in any way utilized by nocturnal lizards such as crested geckos. Compared with other *Rhacodactylus*, which in the wild spend the day in tree hollows, crested geckos spend the day sleeping in the leaves of trees, and it might be assumed that some minimal exposure to sunlight may occur in this more exposed situation. The necessity of sunlight, though, remains to be understood with this species. Captive crested geckos tend to hide when lights are on, and they will not be likely to successfully utilize UV-B. Therefore, UV-B lighting can not be recommended in place of proper supplementation.

Phosphorus and Vitamin A both interact with a lizard's ability to utilize calcium properly. The ratio of calcium to phosphorus should be as close to two parts calcium for every one part of phosphorus, and the ratio of vitamin D_3 to Vitamin A should be one to one. Excess vitamin A can lead to serious health problems. To add to the confusion, zinc is necessary for the transport of Vitamin A. High calcium levels inhibit zinc absorption, and therefore impede the utilization of Vitamin A.

Many geckos store calcium in their endolymphatic sacs. In many species, such as day geckos (*Phelsuma* sp.), these

Although they are exposed to sunlight in nature, there is no evidence that captive crested geckos need ultraviolet light.

chalk sacs (as they are sometimes called) are located on both sides of the neck and will appear as large bulges when full of liquefied calcium carbonate. In *Rhacodactylus*, the sacs are visible as two paired white structures inside the mouth on the palate. Many breeders feel that if these structures appear full, then the geckos are being properly supplemented. This has shown to be far from the case. Obviously, depleted sacs will clearly indicate a problem, though many specimens showing clear symptoms of metabolic bone disease can still appear to have full endolymphatic sacs. Most likely, the gecko may be receiving a proper amount of calcium, yet the body may be unable to utilize it properly due to imbalanced supplementation, such as high or low levels of Vitamin A, Vitamin D_3, etc.

Recommendations

With all the confusion over the best supplementation techniques, it is recommended to find a brand of multivitamin/calcium supplement with ingredients best conforming to the

Supplemented Baby Food Recipe

1/3 of a 2.5oz (about 25 ml) jar turkey baby food

1 6oz (177 ml) jar fruit baby food (banana, apricot, papaya, guava are favorites)

1/2 tsp.(2.5 ml) powdered calcium supplement with vitamin D_3

1/4 tsp. (1.3 ml) powdered multivitamin supplement

Mix all ingredients together thoroughly in a plastic container with a tight-fitting lid and refrigerate. This recipe makes enough to feed a small group of adults or a large group of juveniles for a week. Prepare a new batch every week and discard any unused amounts one week after mixing.

When ready to feed, spoon onto a small dish or lid of a baby food jar. Allow it to warm to room temperature before offering to your geckos. Do not offer more than your geckos will consume within five to six hours.

conditions mentioned above. Preferably, purchase types available in ultra-fine powder, which will work best for dusting crickets. These supplements can also be mixed in pureed diets, with a recommended amount of 1 teaspoon supplementation per 14 oz of pureed food(5ml per 397g).

Dusting crickets with vitamin and calcium supplementation is very important. To dust crickets, select the amount to be fed and place them in a small bucket, tall cup, or other container with tall sides, and sprinkle a little vitamin supplementation over the crickets. Then, gently shake the bucket until the crickets have a fine coating of supplementation visible on them. Finely ground supplements will adhere better to the cricket's exoskeleton than other more gritty types, so try to use a brand that comes in a very fine powder whenever possible.

How Often to Feed?

The frequency of feeding will depend on several factors. For fast growth, hatchlings should be fed daily. While adults can be fed less frequently, breeding animals should be fed more often than pets that are not being bred. Preferably, hatchlings should be offered baby food or other suitable mix (with supplementation) every other day, with supplemented quarter-inch crickets being offered twice per week. Subadult to adult breeding geckos can be offered baby food or other prepared substitutes twice weekly, and offering supplemented crickets twice a week. Opinions vary, and some breeders feed their animals daily, while others feed crickets once a week and pureed food once per week with success.

If you opt for feeding less frequently, you should always monitor your gecko's appearance and body weight. Providing proper supplementation becomes more vital with each feeding. If you feed more often than recommended, obesity may become an issue, especially with nonbreeding geckos. Oversupplementation may possibly cause problems as well.

Water

The importance of misting has already been mentioned in maintaining the proper humidity levels within the cage. Misting cages with spray bottles should be done twice a day for young hatchlings and once a day for adults. When misting, make sure to spray the walls of the cage, plant leaves, etc., so that droplets will form on these surfaces. Some geckos will prefer to lick these droplets up rather than drink from a water bowl. Nevertheless, a water bowl should be provided at all times.

Gargoyle geckos and the other *Rhacodactylus* prefer to lap up water droplets rather than drinking from a bowl.

R. auriculatus prefers to feed more on insects and other prey than on fruits. It tends to eat less fruit than other *Rhacodactylus*.

Water should not be any deeper than the gecko can stand in. Hatchlings can easily drown if they fall in the water bowl and can't touch the bottom of the cup.

Water quality is very important. Municipal water sources may have high levels of potentially toxic chemicals—especially chlorine—and should be avoided. Well-water quality varies from excellent to poor depending on the local conditions, and some may have a high iron or mineral content, which can lead to stains in the cage when misting. The best option would be to purchase a reverse osmosis system for filtering impurities out of your tap water, but bottled distilled water can also be used.

Chapter 5

Breeding

In less than a decade after their rediscovery, crested geckos have quickly become readily affordable. This is due to the breeding efforts of both commercial reptile breeders and hobbyists. Since an individual female can lay 15 to 22 eggs annually, the price of these geckos continues to drop as more and more hatchlings are available each year.

Male crested geckos (right) have a larger swelling behind their vent than females do. This is the hemipenal bulge.

Sexing

If you plan to breed your crested geckos, you need to first make sure you have opposite sexes. It is unfortunate that there is no reliable way to sex juvenile crested geckos, as most individuals offered for sale are immature and therefore unsexed. Some claim to be able to sex immature geckos by the size of their cloacal spurs, or by examining pre-anal pores under magnification, though this has proven unreliable. With several other genera of geckos, cloacal spurs are usually much more pronounced in males than in females. In crested geckos however, comparisons of adult male and female spurs vary greatly, and the same applies to juveniles. Mature, sexed geckos are much more expensive when available, due to the cost of growing them to a sexable size.

With proper care, crested geckos can be visually sexed less than a year after hatching. Sexing is very easy, as the males have very prominent hemipenal bulges immediately after the vent. The hemipenal bulges usually develop suddenly when the gecko is nearing his mature size. Therefore, the size that a male develops hemipenal bulges is not always a reliable indicator that it is mature. If you have two geckos and one has recently developed hemipenal bulges, don't assume that the other similar sized gecko is a female based on the lack of hemipenal bulges. The "female" may surprise you a few weeks later and turn out to be a male as well.

The other clear method for determining the sex of a crested gecko is the presence of pre-anal or femoral pores. These appear as a row of scales with a central pore, extending along the underside of the thighs of mature crested geckos. Both males and females have these pores, though males have very prominent pores compared with those of a female.

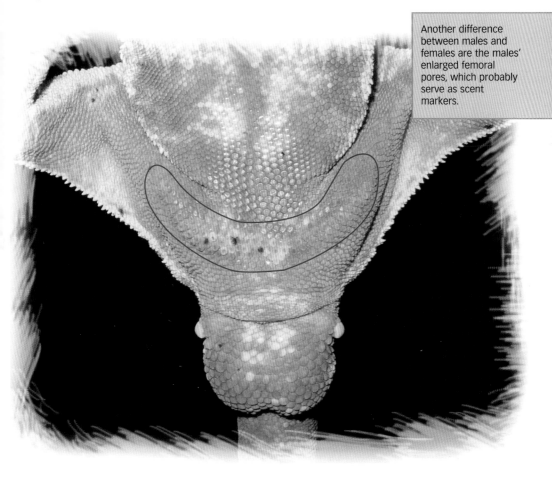

Another difference between males and females are the males' enlarged femoral pores, which probably serve as scent markers.

Maturity

Once geckos reach sexual maturity, males in the same enclosure will usually begin fighting with each other. Though you may never see any actual fighting going on, you may start to notice bite marks on the geckos, usually appearing as faint outlines of gecko jaws on the skin. Sometimes the skin may be broken, especially on the head, and may become infected. If two males continue to be housed together, they will continue fighting, and both geckos will inevitably lose their tails and become unnecessarily stressed due to competition. Always keep mature males separated. Females seem to do fine in group situations and rarely inflict injury on each other.

Setting Up a Breeding Group

Crested geckos don't require any complex preparation for breeding. Unlike many other reptiles from cooler climates, they don't require a cooling period prior to the breeding season. As long as they are kept within their optimum temperature range, fed a proper diet (including vitamin supplementation), and have a suitable laying site, a pair of crested geckos will readily breed without any further needs.

Breeders are attempting to manipulate the size and number of spots on Dalmatian cresteds through selective breeding.

That is not to say that a cooling period isn't beneficial. With males removed from the cage, and three to four months of reduced temperatures, a cool rest period allows the animals some time free of breeding stress and time to replenish their nutritional resources. This should not be a true hibernation, as some reptiles from cooler climates require. Temperatures in the low 70°F range (21 to 22°C) are all that are necessary, with nighttime drops near 60°F (15.6°C) acceptable. The geckos may not eat as much during these cooler periods, and care must be taken to not allow geckos to remain in the low 60°F range for days on end. Any food in their stomachs may not be digested when they are subjected to temperatures in this range, and it will then decompose and cause an internal infection. Daytime temperatures must be allowed to climb back into the low 70°F range in order to ensure for unimpeded digestion and metabolism.

One male may be housed with one or more females continuously. Large scale breeders regularly rotate one male between several cages of females. The male is left in a cage containing multiple females for several days, and then transferred to another cage of females. Usually the male will be very willing to mate once introduced to a new group of females. When housing multiple geckos in a breeding situation, it is important to provide enough hiding places so all individuals can get away from each other to reduce stress.

Courtship and Copulation

Mating usually takes place at night when the animals are more active. During courtship, the male will subdue the female by holding the back of her neck in his mouth. He will then align his body somewhat parallel to hers, and maneuver one of his two hemipenes into her cloacal

Night and Day

Photoperiods (the day/night cycle) are poorly understood in crested geckos. Along with a cooling period, many species of reptiles also react to the reduction of the daylight hours during winter season as part of their seasonal cycling. Since crested geckos are nocturnal, a clear day/night cycle needs to be present for normal functioning. Whether or not cage lighting is used, all lights in the room should be turned off at night. If lights are not used on the cage, the room should not be kept in total darkens during the day. A window or overhead light in the room will be adequate. By providing 12 to 14 hours of daily illumination throughout the year, crested geckos will breed for most of the year. If the photoperiod is reduced, breeding activity could possibly cease. If you plan on having your animals producing during the winter in a room primarily illuminated by light through windows, you should cover up any windows and provide other means of lighting the room. Otherwise, the geckos may sense the shortening of days and discontinue breeding.

opening to deposit sperm. Copulation may continue for several minutes. Afterwards, the female may have visible bite marks on her neck. In most cases, the skin will not be broken, and these marks will disappear the next time the female sheds.

Nesting Sites

A suitable nesting site should be a permanent feature in any enclosure containing breeding geckos. A female can lay a clutch of two eggs every three weeks, and it is best to always be prepared. A nest box can consist simply of a plastic lidded container with an access hole cut in the lid, filled with a moist substrate. Commonly used laying substrates are vermiculite, sphagnum moss, and peat, most of which can be purchased from any plant nursery supply company. Whichever you choose, the substrate must be kept moist but not too wet at all times.

You can make a simple but adequate nest box from a food storage container with a hole cut in the lid. Vermiculite is a commonly used nesting media

Nesting Media

Vermiculite is a granulated, finely layered mineral product that has been heat-treated to expand somewhat, increasing its moisture-holding capabilities. It is normally used as a potting soil additive for moisture retention and soil aeration and is available in different grades from coarse to fine. A medium grade is preferred by most breeders, with individual granules averaging 1/8 inch (0.32 cm) in diameter. With vermiculite, you can mix at a ratio of one part water to two parts vermiculite by weight. Some breeders mix vermiculite by feel. A properly mixed batch of moistened vermiculite will form a clump when a handful is squeezed but will easily break apart when a finger is pushed into the clump. You should not be able to squeeze any traces of excess water out of the clump. Fill the nesting container with enough vermiculite so that it is at least a few inches deep.

Sphagnum moss is a long-fibered moss sold in dry bales. Soak the moss in water until saturated, and then thoroughly squeeze out all excess water. Fill the nesting container a few inches deep with loosely packed moss so the geckos can dig in it easily. When working with sphagnum moss, make sure to wear gloves and avoid inhaling the dry dust, as there is a risk of contracting a fungal infection called *Sporotrichosis*. Spores from this fungus enter cuts in the skin and results in blisters or open sores that can spread to other areas of the body. If spores are inhaled, a serious respiratory infection can result.

Whichever laying substrate you use, it is critical that it is not kept too wet. Crested gecko eggs have a leathery shell which water and gasses freely pass through. If the egg absorbs too much moisture from being in wet nesting material, it will usually die. On the other hand, if the nesting material is too dry, the female may lay her eggs in the only other wet area in the cage—the water bowl—where they will quickly become ruined.

Sperm Retention

As in many reptiles, female crested geckos can retain sperm within their bodies for months. This allows them to produce viable eggs long after an encounter with a male, and may also allow for control of fertilization if the gecko's current environmental or physiological conditions are unsuitable for egg laying. Therefore, don't be surprised if a lone female continues to produce eggs long after she has been removed from a male.

Egg Laying

When the female is ready to lay her eggs, she will dig a hole in the nesting substrate, deposit her clutch of eggs, and then bury them. This process may last for at least an hour or more, and a female who is caught in the act of laying should not be bothered. After burying the eggs, the females provide no further care for them. Normally, females will lay two eggs per clutch, but occasionally only one will be laid.

Egg Collection

You will need to check for eggs at least every few days, so they can be removed to be incubated properly. Carefully dig through the nest box, gently exposing the eggs but not

Check Often

If you have multiple breeding females sharing a nest box, one may uncover another female's eggs when digging her own nesting site. Once exposed, they may quickly dry out if not collected promptly. It is therefore advisable to check the nest boxes in group cages more often than you would for a cage containing one or two females.

altering the position they were laid in. In early stages of development, embryo death may result if the position they were laid in is altered. When you uncover eggs, carefully use a ball-point pen to mark the top surface, and gently lift them, taking care not to turn them. After checking for eggs, add moisture if the substrate has dried out. A spray bottle works well for this purpose. Remember to not overly moisten.

If your breeding animals are kept in a naturalistic planted vivarium, your gecko may end up laying eggs anywhere it feels suitable, even if a designated nesting site is provided. Having this type of setup will make egg collection difficult. If conditions are right, eggs may end up incubating and hatching successfully within the vivarium substrate, but hatchlings could be eaten by their parents if not noticed quickly.

Incubation Methods and Conditions

Once your gecko lays a clutch of eggs, you will need to set them up for incubation. There are many methods that can be used to incubate eggs successfully. Your choice will depend on what method works best for you.

During incubation, you will need to make sure the eggs are provided with a proper temperature, proper moisture, and air circulation. The temperature should remain constant, never fluctuating more than one degree up or down if possible. The recommended temperature for keeping crested geckos—75° to 78°F (23.8 to 25.6°C)—also works well for incubating eggs. The eggs will need to be set in a moistened incubation material, such as perlite or vermiculite. These two substrates are recommended as they retain moisture yet allow air circulation around the eggs. These potting soil additives come in several grades, and a medium to coarse grade should be used.

It is important to make sure the ratio of moisture to vermiculite or perlite is not too wet and not too dry. Many breeders prefer a mixture of one part water to two parts vermiculite or perlite by weight (rather than by volume of either material). Some prefer an even wetter mixture, but it is very important to make sure that the substrate is not too wet, or the eggs will quickly go bad. Since eggs will absorb water from the incubation

Female crested about to lay. She will hold the eggs in her hind feet until the soft shells harden.

substrate, it is critical to use a good quality of water. Reverse osmosis water is preferred if available. Otherwise, avoid using tap water and stick with distilled water.

Actual incubators are not always necessary. If the room your geckos are housed in is kept at a constant, acceptable temperature, then you will be able to incubate your eggs in the room. The eggs will need to be set up in a lidded plastic container filled halfway with moistened incubation substrate. The box can then be put in a secure place in the room.

Air quality is important in maintaining the health of the eggs. Along with moisture, gasses do pass through the egg shell, and if the eggs are kept in stagnant conditions, they will be unable to "breathe" and will die. To allow for air exchange, some breeders will drill several ventilation holes in the sides of the incubation box. This can lead to rapid moisture loss within the egg incubation box, and water will need to be replaced during incubation through misting when necessary. Obviously with this method, it is very difficult to control fluctuations of moisture levels and temperatures.

An easier and more reliable option is to use an airtight plastic incubation box. Since there is no air exchange, the box will need to be manually aerated regularly. The lids should be removed every one or two days, fanning the box several times with the lid to allow for fresh air to permeate into the substrate. When using this method, there is no significant amount of

Temperature Dependent Sex Determination

Many species of reptiles, including a number of species of geckos, have temperature dependent sex determination (TDSD), meaning that the incubation temperature not genetics determines the sex of the offspring. In these species, eggs incubated warmer will produce a greater number of males, while eggs incubated cooler will produce more females. The exact temperatures vary with the species, and some species exhibit slightly different patterns. Most breeders try to incubate at temperatures that result in approximately half males and half females. Some believe that crested geckos and other *Rhacodactylus* species exhibit TDSD, though further study is necessary to confirm this. Incubating at approximately 78°F (26°C) seems to result in a fairly even mixture of sexes.

water loss from the substrate, so moisture replacement should not be necessary if the substrate was mixed properly to begin with. Of course, you should check the incubation substrate periodically to make certain it remains moist.

Incubators can be used, and are necessary if you are unable to maintain a room's temperature within the acceptable range. Most incubators need to be kept in a cool room, which allows the incubator to heat up to the desired temperature. Since all but the most expensive incubators do not have a cooling feature, they will not work in rooms that get hotter than the desired incubation temperature. Air conditioning will be necessary if room conditions are too hot. There are a variety of inexpensive poultry incubators that work well for reptile eggs, and by searching on the Internet you can find instructions on how to build your own incubator out of a variety of readily available materials.

Setting Up the Eggs

When placing eggs in the incubation box, they should be gently set no more than halfway into the substrate. This way, half of the egg is in good contact with the substrate, allowing for absorption of moisture, and half is exposed to allow for air circulation and gas exchange. By placing them halfway into the substrate, the eggs will be less susceptible to rolling around when the box is moved. Remember that eggs should not be turned from the position they were laid in, so transfer the eggs from nest box to incubation box in the position they were laid, and do not disturb for the remainder of incubation.

Before setting up eggs, you should make sure the eggs are fertile. If fertilization was not successful, the female will often lay what is referred to as a slug. A slug has a very different appearance and feel than a fertile egg. Its shell is usually poorly calcified, which gives it a soft rubbery feel and yellowish coloration. The shell of a fertile egg will be firm, leathery in texture, and pure white. A slug is often smaller than and not as plump as a fertile egg.

Though slugs are usually clearly distinguishable from fertile eggs, there are exceptions. Sometimes, an egg that appears fertile on the outside may not have any development taking place internally. These eggs will usually become moldy and begin decomposing a few weeks after being set up for incubation. If you are not clear if an egg is fertile or not, it is best to set it up for incubation and see what happens.

Occasionally eggs may be found that are desiccated. This is the result of eggs being layed in a nesting substrate that is too dry. Often this happens when a group of females is sharing a nest box, and eggs laid by one female are inadvertently dug up when another female is digging her nesting site. Eggs that have sustained significant moisture loss usually are sunken in on at least one side, due to moisture loss through the eggshell. Don't assume the egg is ruined if found in this condition. Often, an egg that appears unrecoverable will absorb water again after being set up in an acceptably moist incubation box, though it may not swell back up to its normal fullness. Though some eggs will not be recoverable, eggs that have lost approximately 40 percent of their moisture have still hatched on numerous occasions without any problems when they are discovered soon enough.

Record Keeping

It is extremely important to keep good records from the time eggs are layed up to when they hatch. Devising a record keeping system and maintaining accurate records are vital to success. Information such as the name or ID number of the female who layed the eggs, date layed, color of parents, etc. should be recorded in some way when the eggs are set up. During the course of incubation, any significant events that arise should be recorded along with the date observed, such as accidental temperature fluctuations, mold problems, changes in egg shape, color, etc. This information can allow you to gradually learn if the conditions you are providing are leading to success or failure. By knowing the date the eggs were layed, you will be able to predict approximately when they will hatch, assuming temperature remains at a suitable level. This will allow you to prepare in advance for housing the hatchlings.

Crested gecko breeders are selecting for interesting and beautiful colors and patterns and combinations of the two. The moonglow variety is pale, almost pearly, in color.

Some breeders will candle their eggs prior to setting up for incubation. This involves shining a light through the egg to visualize the early stages of development. If an egg's position is accidentally disrupted when uncovered in the nest box, candling can help find the correct position to set it up in the incubation box. Fiber-optic light wands used for candling bird eggs also work well for reptile eggs. An alternative to this expensive equipment is a modified flashlight. Simply secure a small cone of dark heavy paper over the end of a flashlight, so the beam is focused through a small hole at the tip of the cone.

Candling is best done in a darkened room. The light is shined through the side of the egg, and the egg is gently rotated to find where embryonic development is taking place. An egg that is only a few days old will look empty inside, except for a reddish round area just under the eggshell on one side, which is known as the blastosphere. This will be the only prominent feature visible at this early stage, and normally appears as a reddish dot surrounded by a thin reddish ring. This is a grouping of cells representing the earliest stages of embryonic development. The egg should be set in the incubation substrate with the blastosphere facing up. The top side of the egg should be gently marked with a ball point pen to make sure eggs don't accidentally get shifted during the incubation period.

Maintenance During Incubation

Eggs should be checked at least every other day for any problems that may arise. Common problems are mold, dehydration, and egg death. Eggs that may not have been fertilized will become discolored in a week or two, and will continue to deteriorate from that point if not noticed early. Sometimes, development within the egg may discontinue, in which case the embryo will die and the egg will also deteriorate.

In the chevron-back variety, the dorsal stripe is broken into distinct bars or chevrons.

Do not discard any egg that begins to change color, develop mold, or otherwise gains an unhealthy appearance until you are sure the egg is clearly dead. Sometimes, mold growth can be easily controlled with a localized application of athlete's foot powder. Mold growth on the eggshell doesn't always affect the egg internally if controlled early. Sometimes, an egg may turn a dark yellowish-brown color and appear like it is rotting, but if it is not "sweating" fluid, it may still be healthy on the inside and hatch without problems. Only discard an egg when it appears to be sweating or leaking discolored fluid, develops an odor, or if it becomes so moldy and shriveled up that there is clearly no hope of its continued survival.

You should check at least once daily to make sure the proper temperature is being maintained. Temperature fluctuations should be avoided, as this could lead to developmental problems.

Depending on the type of incubation setup, you may need to monitor the moisture levels in the incubation box, especially if you have ventilation holes in the incubation box. Moisture should be added with a spray bottle. In sealed boxes without holes, moisture loss will be very minimal, and should not require any additional water replacement for the duration of incubation. Again, the latter method is recommended due to the reduced potential for problems resulting from fluctuating moisture levels. Humidity levels within the egg box should remain at about 80 to 90 percent.

Aeration is critical to prevent stagnant conditions in the incubation box. With airtight incubation boxes, it is necessary to aerate the box daily by removing the lid to allow for air exchange. This also provides an opportunity for inspection of the eggs. If using a box with holes, there will be some aeration, but the lid should still be removed from the incubation box every few days to ensure a thorough air exchange.

Preparation for Hatchlings

When incubating eggs at 78°F (26°C), crested gecko eggs usually will hatch in an average of 56 to 60 days. Expect incubation to last longer when the eggs are incubated in cooler conditions and to be shorter in warmer conditions. It is not good to incubate at a higher temperature to reduce the waiting period, as severe developmental

Crested gecko pipping its eggs. The baby gecko may stay in the egg for a few hours or even a day after pipping.

Yolk Attached

Rarely, a hatchling may be found with remains of a yolk sac still attached to the gecko by the umbilical cord. When this is found, place the hatchling in a small cage with several layers of paper towels on the bottom, lightly misted with room temperature water to prevent the yolk sac from sticking to the substrate. Usually within 24 hours, the yolk sac will have fallen off, in which case the umbilical scar should be gently inspected to make sure it healed over properly. When everything appears normal, the gecko can be returned to its normal cage.

problems can result. Once you predict when hatching will take place, it is best to have a cage set up in advance, along with a source of suitably sized crickets available.

Hatching & Hatchlings

When you are expecting hatchlings, keep an eye out for slits cut in the eggshell when you check the incubation box. This is made by the hatchling gecko's egg tooth. Each baby gecko will have this tiny pointed scale on the upper lip used to slice through the tough eggshell. This egg tooth is lost after the gecko's first shed. The process of slitting open the eggshell is called pipping.

After the crested gecko pips, it will take a long time for the hatchling to finally emerge from the egg. It may often sit there for hours with only its head or just the tip of its nose protruding from the slit, occasionally appearing to be struggling. Though this is an exciting

One small step: a crested gecko leaves the egg.

Strive for Simplicity

It is best to keep cage setup simple for hatchlings. Newspaper or paper towels are best used as substrate for hatchlings. A shallow water bowl should be provided. Items to climb on should be included, such as branches, bamboo sections, lengths of PVC pipe, or even small potted plants. Just remember to not overdo it.

time, avoid the temptation to help it out of the egg or otherwise disturb the hatchling. The gecko will still be attached to its yolk sac via the umbilical cord, and it is critical that the gecko absorbs the remaining yolk into its body before it leaves the egg. If you pull the gecko out of the egg prematurely, the process becomes disrupted and death may result. Be patient, it may take many hours to a full day from the time it pips to the time it finally emerges from the egg. Avoid the urge to constantly check on the hatchling's progress, as the constant disturbance may delay the process even longer.

Once the gecko is finally out of the egg, it is time to set it up in his new home. Obviously, crested gecko hatchlings are tiny and very fragile. Never pick them up or restrain them by the tails, as they will easily come off. The safest way to pick them up is to gently coax the hatchling onto your hand and transfer it immediately to his cage. Never handle a crested gecko hatchling any more than absolutely necessary. Once securely in its cage, the hatch date should be recorded.

Housing Hatchlings

Since hatchlings are very tiny in size, they should be set up in cages that are not too large. Small plastic cages available from pet stores for housing small animals are perfect for housing one or two hatchlings. Small, lidded plastic storage containers or large, clear plastic gallon jars with air holes will also work well. A 10-gallon aquarium (38 l) with a screen lid will easily hold up to ten hatchlings for a few months. The key is to give them enough room to get away from each other, yet not have a cage so expansive that it becomes difficult for these small geckos to search for food. The chances of hatchlings tracking down small crickets or a dab of fruit mixture get smaller as the cage gets larger. Make sure the lid to the cage fits snugly, as these tiny hatchlings can squeeze thorough the smallest gaps. Avoid setting up hatchlings in a lushly planted vivarium, as they will get lost in the vegetation, making it difficult to monitor their condition.

Proper Care of Hatchlings

A small shallow water bowl should be provided at all times. Though hatchlings seem to

Crested geckos and other *Rhacodactylus* species shed their skins shortly after hatching.

prefer drinking water droplets off the side of the cage after misting, they will use a bowl as well. Hatchlings can easily drown in overfilled water containers, so make sure to only provide a thin film of water on the bottom of the bowl.

Humidity, along with good ventilation, is extremely important for hatchlings, more so than with adults. Hatchlings will shed soon after hatching and shed much more often than will adults. Exposure to a dry environment will cause serious shedding problems. Cage walls should be misted twice daily, more often in very dry surroundings. Ambient relative humidity should be kept around 75 percent and good cage ventilation is a must to prevent stagnation that can lead to moldy surroundings.

Hatchlings of the same age can be kept in groups, but they must be given enough room to hide from each other. Most importantly, hatchlings housed together must always be similarly sized. Even if cagemates are the same age, they will often grow at different rates, and there will usually be noticeable size discrepancies after growing for a month or so. Those that grow faster will be outcompeting the smaller, slower-growing cagemates for food. When this is noticed, the smaller individuals should be separated out into their own cages. If this resizing is not kept up with during the growout period, the smaller ones will often become stressed to the point that they begin loosing weight. Never expect to keep a group together in the same cage from the time they hatch until maturity. Be prepared for differing growth rates with extra cages set up for the smaller ones.

Feeding and supplementation is the same as for adults, though hatchlings should be fed more often and obviously smaller amounts. Fruit puree or baby food with vitamin supplementation mixed in should be offered daily as a small dab presented on a small dish or piece of a paper plate. Offer only a quantity that will be consumed overnight, as it will quickly become moldy if left for longer periods. Be sure to remove the serving plate the following day so any residue will not lead to mold growth. Crested gecko hatchlings can get stuck in larger servings of fruit puree if they walk through it, and if they get it on their toes, it will also limit their ability to climb.

Small crickets dusted with vitamin supplement should be offered every other day. Hatchlings will be able to easily eat quarter-inch (0.64 cm) crickets. Make sure to have a steady supply of appropriately sized crickets. Only add the number or crickets that your geckos will be able to consume within several hours. Too many crickets in a cage can stress the inhabitants. After a while, you should be able to develop a feel for how many crickets and how much fruit to offer with every feeding to avoid having excess left over the following day.

Genotype vs. Phenotype

The terms genotype and phenotype often come up when discussing the selective breeding of animals. The two terms are different but related. The genotype is the actual genetic makeup of an organism, as distinguished from its physical appearance. The phenotype is the observable physical and/or biochemical characteristics of an organism, as determined by genetics and environmental factors. So, the genotype determines the phenotype.

Selective Breeding

Over the short period of time since crested geckos were introduced to the herpetological community, a wide variety of colors, patterns, and combinations of color and pattern have developed. Some of these have randomly cropped up, while others have been intentionally bred to emphasize these traits. New and interesting forms continue to emerge, making the future of crested gecko color and pattern morphs something to look forward to.

Many species of reptiles have been selectively bred to emphasize visible traits, including corn snakes, ball pythons, leopard geckos, and bearded dragons. These species are now available in seemingly every possible combination of color and pattern. The list of names for all these color morphs is longer than the number of existing phenotypes. Some breeders will often put a name on something that is just a slight variation from the typical color form and hope that collectors will want it and pay a hefty price.

For example, corn snake coloration varies considerably depending on where in the United States the individual is found. If amelanism (lack of melanin, a black pigment) is introduced to a number of corns from different localities, the eventual resulting amelanistic offspring will look drastically different. Some will be mostly dark reddish orange with white markings; others will be more yellow with white markings. Still others will be lacking more white than others, etc. Some would just be likely to call all of these amelanistic and accept that they can be variable, but others, looking to cater to the collector, would want to name every different variation, leading to confusion among hobbyists on where to draw the line between phenotypes that seems to run together.

Crested geckos seem to be going down the same path. New variants are popping up all the time, and it is impossible to keep up with all the names that breeders and hobbyists give them. Some, like the Dalmatian phase, will probably always remain static, unless someone decides to delineate those that have larger or more numerous spots than others.

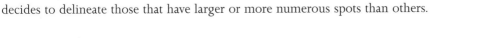

The flame morph has light markings on the back and sides. This flame is particularly brightly colored.

This individual may best be described as brick red with high contrast markings.

Some breeders try to keep it simple and refer to two types of crested gecko colors. One is the normal or patternless form, which is usually plain yellow to tan to reddish brown in coloration, with a minimal amount of light highlights. The other form would be the flame or fire morph, in which the gecko has a well-defined stripe of contrasting bright yellow or orange color on his back and head, along with side markings, among other features. The flame form is usually more desirable than the normal form and, therefore, more expensive.

Due to the variability of crested geckos, others would tend to break the normals down into a multitude of colors, and the flames could be divided into even larger number of morphs. Normals have been split down to various types, such as buckskin, orange, red, and yellow. Sulfurs would be ones that are exceedingly bright yellow. Chocolate would refer to those with dark brown coloration. Moonglow has been given to those that are a very pale grayish tan in coloration.

Flames have been assigned different names reflecting distinguishing features present in the patterning. Pinstripes are those that have bright contrasting lines bordering the dorsal stripe, extending in an unbroken paired line down to the base of the tail. Harlequins are those flames

Starting a Selective Breeding Project

In order to manage a selective breeding project, you will need to be able to keep accurate and detailed records. Since hatchlings will not often show their best colors, you will need space to grow out all offspring until they are of a size where they are displaying their ultimate colors, at which point you would need to find homes for those not meeting your standards.

One danger of selective breeding is the possibility of inbreeding. This is not usually a problem in early stages of breeding closely related geckos to each other, but it can eventually be a problem down the road if new genetics aren't being regularly added to keep future generations genetically diverse. Results of inbreeding are most noticeably developmental deformations, though seemingly normal appearing yet inbred animals may have other less noticeable undesirable features, including impaired fertility or weak health.

For best results, make sure you are working with a diverse initial stock from the beginning. Select as many females as you can that display the traits you want to work toward emphasizing, and breed the best males you can find with these traits. Try to do your best to obtain females from various sources. Even though all crested geckos in captivity go back to a small number of initial collections, enough mixing and matching appears to have kept the genetics of today's offspring strong. One male can easily be bred to at least 10 females, therefore creating a genetically diverse assemblage of offspring. It is important to keep records on the parentage of the offspring, as you will want to avoid regular inbreeding in one lineage. Breeding two exceptionally colored siblings together, or breeding a hatchling to his/her parent, is unlikely to cause problems, but care must be taken to not keep breeding resulting generations together again. Mixing new genetics into the project, known as out-breeding, is very beneficial.

with high amounts of light patterning on the sides and legs in addition to the dorsal side. Chevron-backs are those in which the dorsal stripe is broken at intervals down the back, giving the illusion on some (but not all) specimens of a row of chevron patterns running down the back. Tigers are those with reduced dorsal striping, and have emphasized dark bands encircling the body. They also often have patterned undersides. Fringeds will have the webbing of their hind legs outlined in a contrasting white to yellow color.

This gecko has both tiger and harlequin traits.

As breeders continue to mix and match the various phenotypes, more and more variants will be produced, and more names will be given. Rather than go on the names given to you by the seller, it is best to just pick the colors you prefer in person, rather than be disappointed over confusion generated from a multitude of names for similar morphs.

Many of the different colors seen in other species of reptiles are due to various combinations of genetic mutations, such as amelanism/albinism (lacking black pigment), hypomelanism (reduction of black pigment), leucisism (snowy white with fully pigmented eyes), and anerythrism (lack of red pigment). These recessive traits are inheritable only when both mates possess the same genes for that trait, though they don't visibly show the trait themselves.

Though unknown in current collections, it is still possible for some desirable genetic mutations to pop up at random. Normally, traits like albinism that unexpectedly crop up in captive breeding are due to the chance combination of two normally appearing animals that are gene carriers for the trait. Though the genetics for all crested geckos in captivity today go back to a limited number of collections, it is still possible that the genes for something like amelanism are out there in a few animals, and all that is needed is the chance occurrence that the two are bred together. If any albinos or other genetic mutations are ever produced, they will initially sell for a very high price.

It is fun to experiment with selective breeding in hopes of eventually emphasizing a trait in future generations. Basically, two geckos of similar desired color or pattern are bred together to hopefully produce a number of offspring displaying the same trait. Of these offspring, the best examples are selected and bred together, resulting in hatchlings with an even better appearance to them. Once the particular trait is refined to one's liking, other traits can be introduced in the same manner. If all works as it is hoped, eventually a gecko displaying a combination of the traits will be produced.

Despite the new forms and variations constantly appearing, it is not yet understood if selective breeding will work easily for all traits. Blending of colors and patterns clearly occurs, yet

This is a fine example of a red phase crested.

This gecko might be considered a Dalmatian crested, but its spots are much larger than in a typical Dalmatian.

selectively breeding similarly colored individuals may not reliably produce mirror images of the parents. A certain percentage may reflect the desired qualities, yet a portion of the offspring may in no way resemble the parent's color or pattern. Considering the numbers of variations that occur today are all derived from a relatively small number of individuals, it is assumed that this species is polymorphic, with each individual capable of producing a variety of different appearing offspring. It is in no way meant to discourage selective breeding, as some pattern or color traits may just be more likely to be intensified using this method than others. Until more systematic experimentation is done, the genetics of crested gecko color and pattern remain unclear. Perhaps the combination of two traits will yield something completely new and unexpected.

Aside from color and pattern, other visible traits might be selectively bred for. These include geckos with the spiny crest that runs the length of the body to the pelvic region, instead of fading out in the center of the back. Another trait that might be bred for are those with crests that are exceptionally wide, forming lobes that actually stick out some distance on either side of the head, creating a very angular, rhombic shaped head. These characteristics, combined with the trait for brightly colored crest margins, would make for an excellent breeding project.

Gargoyle geckos are being captive bred in fairly good numbers and selection for interesting patterns and bright colors is beginning to show results.

Chapter 6

Crested Gecko Health

Crested geckos are durable animals that don't seem to come down with as many health problems as some other commonly kept reptiles do. As long as they are properly kept, a crested gecko can live a long life in captivity. Many common health problems are the result of inadequate care, the most common being nutritional imbalance.

Finding a Reptile Vet

A good way to find a vet educated in reptile medicine is to search the listings of members on the web page of the Association of Reptile and Amphibian Veterinarians (ARAV). The web site for the ARAV is www.arav.org. There you can find the closest vet to you who is a member, and therefore, up to date on the latest in proper reptile care. The ARAV is dedicated to improving reptilian veterinary care and husbandry through research and education. If you have a local herpetological society, they may be able to recommend a vet to you, as well.

Before problems arise, you should seek out a veterinarian with reptile experience in your area. Unfortunately, veterinarians with any knowledge of proper reptile husbandry and medicine are few and far between. This has been slowly changing, as reptiles have become more popular and accepted as pets in recent years. Pet stores that sell reptiles can often recommend veterinarians, as well as fellow hobbyists in your area. It is worth traveling the extra distance for good care and advice that may otherwise mean life or death for your pet.

As pet reptiles become increasingly popular, the number of veterinarians with at least basic knowledge of reptile medicine continues to grow. Still, it is a difficult task to find a veterinarian with proper experience. Many vets still specialize only in traditional pets, such as dogs and cats and other popular warm-blooded animals. Don't necessarily go to a vet who may claim to have experience treating reptiles, as their experiences may be very limited. The many negative experiences from keepers clearly show that there are too many vets who accept reptile patients yet really don't know what they are doing, despite their good intentions. With diligent searching, you can find vets that are knowledgeable. Even the experts may not have the answers to everything, as herpetological medicine has, until recently, been an area that has not received enough attention.

Quarantine

All new acquisitions should always be housed singly and kept away from any other reptiles in your possession for at least three months. This is preferably done in a separate room, and supplies should not be shared between quarantine animals and the rest of the collection. Always take care of isolated animals last, and sanitize your hands afterwards.

Quarantine allows for any potentially communicable problems to develop away from the main collection. The health of animals in quarantine should be closely monitored during this time. Some breeders administer prophylactic dosages of medications that target parasitic worms and protozoans. Deparasitizing should only be performed under the supervision of a veterinarian experienced with reptile medicine.

Since all crested geckos in captivity are captive born, the likelihood that parasites will be present is greatly reduced. However, housing these clean animals in close proximity to wild-caught or otherwise sick animals (or sharing supplies between sick and healthy animals) greatly increases the risk of pathogen spread.

Stress

As with humans, stress in crested geckos can result from any uncomfortable experience. By meeting all the requirements needed by this species, problems with stress should not be an issue. Though your gecko may not show it, you should assume that certain unavoidable events, like handling and egg laying, are stressful to some degree. It is the owner's responsibility to make sure these uncomfortable times are kept to a minimum, and that the gecko is kept happy by providing all that it needs for a healthy existence.

No matter how calm your gecko is, handling does cause some stress and should be kept to a minimum. Subadult giant gecko pictured.

Negative situations that continue for a long period of time will lead to health problems such as loss of appetite, which will then progress to emaciation and death if the problem is not corrected.

The proliferation of some internal parasites may be stress induced. A healthy immune system normally keeps the parasite load suppressed to harmless levels, but when stressed the parasites quickly multiply and overtake the animal, causing death if not treated.

Keep in mind that shipping and transporting geckos is extremely stressful. Consider how much the carriers throw the packages around, as well as the many temperature and humidity fluctuations experienced along the way and the lack of food and water. When receiving geckos that have been shipped to you, make sure to set them up in a suitable environment as soon as possible, offer drinking water, and leave them alone for a few days to settle down and adjust to the new surroundings.

Physical hazards

Crested geckos (and feeder insects) should be kept away from potentially toxic substances. Cigarette smoke is obviously bad for humans and can be worse for reptiles. Chemical fumes, such as those produced from aerosol insecticides and household cleaners, should not be used in the same room as crested geckos. After using cleaning chemicals to clean cages or cage furnishings, make sure to thoroughly rinse all residues off so they are not accidentally licked up by your geckos.

Injuries can be avoided by making sure all cages and their furnishings are safe. Make sure there are no rough-cut materials in the cage. Burrs on rough-cut edges can catch toes or flaps of skin and create tears. Edges of hardware cloth or metal screen can be sharp, and should not be within reach of geckos. Make sure your geckos are unable to come in direct contact with hot light bulbs. Be sure there are no electrical wires or components exposed in the cage. Materials such as rocks, driftwood, or other heavy objects need to be secured so they don't move. These materials can shift and fall, injuring or even killing an inhabitant.

Tail Loss

Tail loss is probably the most common problem experienced by keepers. Tails are easily broken off during rough handling, and the gecko is even able to voluntarily drop the tail as a defensive reaction to certain

Note the bite marks from a cagemate on this gecko's head. Most bites are superficial and do not require treatment.

situations, an ability known as autotomy. When removed from the body, the tail will reflexively wiggle for quite a while. When being pursued by predators in the wild, a crested gecko is able to drop its tail, which theoretically will turn the attention of the attacker to the tail, allowing the gecko to escape from the now distracted predator.

Nearly all adult crested geckos found in the wild lack tails. Most keepers, however, dislike the appearance of a crested gecko without a tail, to the point that breeders often have difficulty selling tailless specimens. Tail loss can be prevented through gentle handling. Never restrain a crested gecko by the tail. Avoid stressful situations that may cause a gecko to drop its tail.

This gecko has a small wound on its head. Eliminating sharp edges from the enclosure will help prevent geckos from getting wounds.

Geckos who lose their tails will normally recover without incident, as long as the gecko isn't living in an unsanitary environment that could lead to infection. Unlike some species of lizards, crested geckos will not regenerate their tails.

Superficial Injuries

External injuries such as skin lacerations and bites usually heal without any problems as long as the cage is kept clean to prevent conditions that can lead to infection. Injuries should be monitored closely, and if infections appear, you should see your veterinarian immediately.

Common Health Problems
Shedding Problems

Dysecdysis is the inability to shed some or all of the skin, which leads to other serious problems. With crested geckos, the retained skin will usually have a dull, somewhat wrinkled appearance. The skin may be flaking off in areas, yet difficult to manually remove. A gecko with retained skin all over his body will be unlikely to eat until the skin has been removed. It may also display an inability to move naturally or climb vertical surfaces. An affected gecko that is left untreated will likely die.

Sometimes the skin will be successfully shed on the body, but will be retained on the feet and legs. If not caught in time, the skin may tighten and constrict the limb, restricting blood flow to the extremity and resulting in loss of the limb.

Dysecdysis can be caused by a number of things, but most often results from dehydration and/or low ambient humidity. Skin may also be retained at the site of a skin abrasion, bite, or burn.

To treat dysecdysis, you will need to asses the condition of the gecko first. If it is in advanced stages, veterinary aid may be necessary. If it is caught early, the problem can be corrected with no ill effects. Isolate the affected gecko in a small deli cup with plenty of ventilation holes in the sides, with either damp sphagnum moss or moistened paper towels as a substrate. Several hours in this humid enclosure often loosens the dried skin, which can then be peeled off manually. When removing shed skin, be very careful to remove all skin from around feet and toes, as well as the covering of skin over the eyes. Sometimes,

This crested is about to shed. After a shed cycle, make sure no pieces of skin adhere to your pet.

Signs of an Unhealthy Gecko

If your geckos displays any of the signs in the list below, it may need veterinary attention. If you are in doubt, it is better to seek the opinion of a veterinarian with experience in reptile medicine than to wait and see what happens. The sooner the animal sees the vet, the greater the chance it will recover.

- refusing food—can be caused by temperature extremes
- sunken eyes
- abnormal feces—runny, odd color, excessive odor, worms
- listless or sluggish behavior—can be caused by cool temperatures
- weight loss
- vomiting
- shedding problems—especially if skin is constricting toes, feet, or limbs
- inability to climb or adhere to vertical surfaces
- inability to right itself when turned upside down

especially on the belly, retained skin is difficult to differentiate from shed areas without close inspection. Small forceps are useful in removing shed skin.

Dehydration

Dehydration usually occurs due to mistreatment. As long as a gecko is offered water and proper humidity levels, dehydration will never be an issue. Geckos weakened from sickness or injury may not actively seek out water, and therefore may need to be manually offered moisture. Some geckos may prefer to lick up droplets of water from misting rather than drink out of a bowl, so you will need to observe your animals and adjust your methods as needed.

Metabolic Bone Disease

Metabolic bone disease (MBD) results from the gecko's inability to properly utilize calcium, usually occurring in animals receiving infrequent or no supplementation or improperly balanced supplementation. Bones will become decalcified and soft, exposing the gecko to increased risk of injury. The animal will become weak, mobility will be impaired, and various parts of the body may become disfigured.

Some symptoms of MBD include a jutting lower jaw, a soft flexible lower jaw, inability to walk or climb, limb disfigurement, and kinks in the spine and/or tail.

Calcium sacs, two of which are located on the roof of a crested gecko's mouth, will appear white when containing calcium reserves, and empty when not receiving enough calcium. Just because calcium is present in the calcium sacs doesn't mean all is necessarily well. An imbalance of nutrients that aid in the utilization of calcium may result in MBD.

Geckos in the early stages of MBD can recover when the use of proper supplements is implemented. Advanced symptoms require the care of a vet, and the most severe cases may not be reversible.

Floppy tail syndrome is a poorly understood condition that may be nutritional, genetic, or behavioral in origin.

Floppy Tail Syndrome

Floppy tail syndrome is a poorly understood condition that is observed in captive arboreal lizards that spend a great deal of time on vertical surfaces with the head pointing downward. Normally when in this position, the tail will be laying flat against the vertical surface, pointing upward. A gecko with floppy tail syndrome will be unable to hold his tail up when in this position and the tail will flop down over the back.

This condition has been blamed on nutritional deficiencies and is considered by some to be a symptom of metabolic bone disease. Animals with this condition may not ever display any other symptoms of MBD, and therefore this condition can not necessarily be attributed to MBD. Further study of the condition is needed.

To prevent floppy tail syndrome from happening, some breeders recommend having a suitable balance of horizontal and vertical surfaces, so the geckos aren't forced to always be on the vertical walls of the cage, which might create strain on the tail.

Spinal, Pelvic, or Tail Kinks

This is another problem often considered a symptom of metabolic bone disease or improper supplementation. Some geckos are born with kinks in their spine, pelvis, or tail, while others appear to develop kinks in later stages of growth. Some kinks may not be noticeable until the gecko gets larger, while other kinks seem to suddenly appear closer to adulthood.

Skeletal kinks may be the result of MBD, but some geckos may not display other symptoms of this disease. Until further studies confirm this, we need to consider other possibilities. Lack of genetic diversity in some colonies may result in inbreeding, which can possibly create deformities, such as spinal kinks.

Kinks are normally irreversible once noticed, but the animals may continue with a seemingly healthy existence. Some may even breed successfully, though this is not recommended in case inbreeding is a factor in this condition. Geckos with abdominal or pelvic kinks may experience trouble passing eggs through these areas.

Egg Binding

When a female is unable to pass her eggs from her body, she is referred to as being egg bound. The causes of egg binding (also known as dystocia) are poorly known, but the condition is often attributed to nutritional deficiencies or lack of a suitable laying site. Eggs that are not laid at the appropriate time will solidify and harden within the female's abdomen and will be easily felt through the underside of her body.

The outlook is normally bleak for an egg-bound female. Once the eggs are hardened, they will not be able to be passed. Surgical removal has been performed successfully on other species of reptiles, but the cost of this procedure can be prohibitive. An egg-bound female can live for quite a while with this condition, but her health will continue to deteriorate. Prevention through proper nutrition and providing a suitable nest box is the best course of action.

Prolapse of Cloaca

The term prolapse is defined as the falling or slipping of an organ out of its proper place. In the case of the cloaca, the rear portion of the intestine passes out the vent. This condition occurs for a number of reasons, some of which are not fully understood. Egg-bound females trying to pass eggs can sometimes end up prolapsing their cloaca. Abdominal injury can also create this problem, and other times there is no apparent cause. Consult with your veterinarian as soon as possible should your gecko experience this problem.

An egg bound female gecko. Having a suitable nesting site available usually prevents egg binding.

Prolapse of Hemipenis

Occasionally a male crested gecko will be unable to withdraw one of his two hemipenes back into his body after copulation. Sometimes this can be due to a piece of vermiculite or other foreign material getting stuck to the organ preventing it from retracting, while other times there is no clear cause.

If caught early, the hemipenis can sometimes be massaged back into the body by experienced breeders. This is difficult to accomplish and may not always be completely successful depending on how long the hemipenis has been prolapsed. Often the problem is caught after the hemipenis becomes necrotic, and it must be amputated by a veterinarian. This does not prevent mating, as the gecko can use his other hemipene.

Regurgitation

Regurgitation can occur as a result of rough handling (especially soon after feeding), extreme temperature changes after feeding, internal parasites, or any stressful situation. See your vet if regurgitation becomes a problem.

Emergency Prolapse Treatment

If you find your male crested gecko with a hemipenal prolapse, there are a few steps you should take to prevent any further injury or infection. If it appears to be a fresh prolapse, with a healthy pink color and with no swelling, you can attempt to put it back in the body by trying these methods:

- Wash any debris adhering to the hemipenis with lukewarm water. Carefully inspect the cloacal opening to see if there are any visible foreign objects that may be preventing the hemipenis from retracting and carefully remove them with forceps. If the hemipenis doesn't slowly retract after cleaning, proceed to the next step.
- Turn on the sink slightly so there is a thin stream of cold water coming out of the tap. Direct the stream of water on the organ, and run cold water on it for several minutes without getting the water on the rest of the body. If successful, the hemipenis will slowly withdraw back into the body during contact with the cold water.
- Some breeders and keepers have had success treating prolapse in other reptiles by soaking the hemipenis in a strong solution of sugar in cool water. You can certainly try this with your *Rhacodactylus* if the other two methods do not resolve the problem.

If you are unable to get the hemipenis to retract, it will eventually become necrotic, turn black, and dry up. Sometimes you may not notice a prolapse until it is at this stage, which happens within a few days. It is best to have a qualified veterinarian amputate the hemipenis as early as possible to avoid any unnecessary discomfort to the animal and reduce any possibility of infection.

Diarrhea

A very common problem with crested geckos is runny feces. This is usually a problem with geckos that are offered a predominantly pureed diet without any roughage obtained from crickets and other material. Though some don't believe it is a problem and have bred crested geckos successfully with runny stools, it is recommended to offer a good balance of crickets and pureed food to maintain solid feces.

Regardless of whether runny stool are considered a health problem or not, it becomes a difficult chore to clean cages with liquefied feces dried on the walls of the cage. Solid fecal pellets are much easier to pick off the cage, and create less of an aesthetic problem in glass enclosures.

Intestinal Impactions

Large indigestible objects or an accumulation of small indigestible objects can become lodged in the intestine, restricting flow of waste and ultimately causing death if not passed. Occasionally, crested geckos may get a mouthful of substrate when they pounce on a cricket, which will then be swallowed. Fresh hatchling crested geckos left in incubation boxes for over a day have ingested vermiculite granules which have lead to fatal impactions.

Impactions may be clearly noticeable if the ingested object(s) are fairly large, but unfortunately

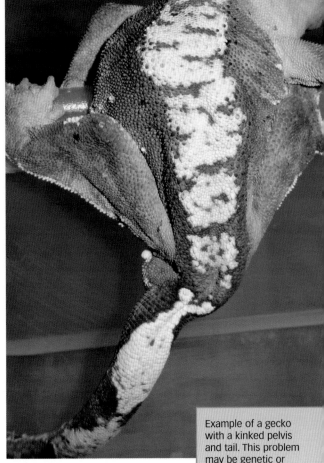

Example of a gecko with a kinked pelvis and tail. This problem may be genetic or nutritional.

most impactions are not noticed until a necropsy is performed to determine the cause of death.

Since impactions are difficult to diagnose until it is too late, it is best to do everything you can to prevent the possibility of it happening to your gecko. Make sure to use substrates that are small enough to be passed if accidentally ingested. Avoid granular substrates such as gravel or anything else that can fit into the gecko's mouth. Impactions may also result from feeding insects with thick exoskeletons such as beetles. Though healthy adult geckos seem to pass vermiculite without any problems, younger juveniles can't. It is especially important to not allow hatchlings to sit in egg incubation boxes full of perlite or vermiculite for more than a day, as they have been known to ingest these materials and become impacted after being in the box a few days.

Weight Loss and Emaciation

Geckos will often respond to stress or sickness by not eating, which will lead to weight loss if the problem is not corrected. Internal parasites can also cause emaciation. Usually the first signs of emaciation are clearly visible pelvic bones and a noticeable thinness to the neck region. See your vet if the cause of the weight loss is not readily apparent and correctable, such as inappropriate temperatures.

Bacterial Infections

As with all animals, any open wound has the potential to become infected if conditions allow. Usually minor wounds heal very quickly without incident if the gecko is healthy and kept in a clean environment. Regularly check any wounds to make sure problems aren't developing and treat as necessary. Topical antibiotic cream can be sparingly used on infected injuries. Apply the cream to the affected area, and then lightly wipe off any excess. Avoid using liberal amounts of antibiotic cream on injuries.

Bacterial infections can also occur internally. This is more difficult to diagnose, and a veterinarian will be needed to identify and treat. Usually, an internal bacterial infection is not noticeable until a necropsy is performed on an animal that has succumbed to the infection. There are rarely any external signs that indicate an internal bacterial infection. The exception would be an infection of the digestive tract, which your veterinarian would discover through fecal examinations. If your gecko is lethargic, losing weight, or otherwise doesn't appear healthy, see your vet as soon as possible.

Obesity

Obesity is usually a problem only with nonbreeding, well-fed animals. Close monitoring of your gecko's weight and adjustment of feeding frequency will help prevent obesity. An obese gecko in a breeding group is most likely not producing.

Parasites

Compared with other commonly kept lizards, crested geckos are affected by a minimal number of parasites. Determining the presence of internal parasites is performed by analyzing a fresh fecal sample under a microscope. This is a job best left to an experienced veterinarian. Rarely will a fecal sample from any captive reptile be perfectly devoid of any microorganisms. There are normal populations of bacteria and protozoans that live within the bodies of reptiles, some of which are beneficial and aid in digestion, while others are parasitic yet are maintained at harmless levels by the immune system. Some inexperienced veterinarians want to treat a reptile for anything noticed in a fecal sample. Some antiparasitics are harsh on the body, and improper dosages can cause death. An experienced reptile veterinarian will properly identify unhealthy levels of parasitic organisms and will be familiar with the best methods of treatment. There are disagreements in the developing field of herpetological medicine, and additional research is necessary to understand and better treat a number of common reptile parasites.

Protozoans

These unicellular organisms are the most commonly encountered parasites in crested geckos. In most cases, they inhabit the digestive system and are often readily noticeable in fecal samples viewed under a microscope. Rarely have crested geckos been observed with serious protozoan infestations. If observed, unhealthy populations of protozoans should be treated with appropriate antiparasitics as recommended by your veterinarian.

Cryptosporidiosis is a life-threatening condition caused by the protozoan organism *Cryptosporidium sp.* In species that affect reptiles, this parasite lives in the digestive system, and during part of its life cycle, it encases itself in the lining of the intestine and/or stomach. Large infestations can severely inflame these organs and disrupt digestion, ultimately leading to death. In collections of certain species, especially leopard geckos, *Cryptosporidium* infections are feared by keepers more than any other pathogen. Cryptosporidiosis in leopard geckos may possibly be stress induced, though little research has been done to better understand this prevalent parasite.

An unidentified species of *Cryptosporidium* has been found in a number of individual crested geckos fecal samples (J. Hiduke, Personal Communication), but none of these geckos ever developed symptoms of cryptosporidiosis. Whether or not this species of *Cryptosporidium* is a serious threat to crested geckos will remain unknown until further research is done.

Worms

Parasitic worms, especially pinworms, are sometimes found in the digestive tract of various lizards in captivity. Though they may be observed rarely in some individuals, worms are generally not a problem with crested geckos. An experienced veterinarian can determine the presence of worms with fecal samples and can treat them with antihelminthics.

External Parasites

With many species of reptiles, mites can become a serious problem. The black snake mite, *Ophionyssus natricis*, is a most dreaded external parasite, since infestations can be spread easily, are difficult to control, and can cause extreme discomfort and even kill reptiles. This species of mite usually affects snakes and large-scaled lizards such as blue-tongue skinks. Fortunately, geckos are not the preferred host for black mites, and they should never be a problem for the crested gecko keeper.

There are a few mites that affect geckos, especially a species of red mite. Some types of mites are not bloodsucking and only live on dead skin, while others may be parasitic. Regardless, these mites should not be allowed to persist, and should be removed by rubbing the gecko with a cotton swab dipped in vegetable oil. These mites often accumulate in the armpits and any other minimally exposed areas. *Rhacodactylus auriculatus* even has "mite pockets" on the undersides of their thighs. In the wild, these structures provide optimum conditions and are packed full of red mites. The function of these mite pockets, which occur on a

Crested with a necrotic tail tip, probably from an infected wound. Keep an eye out for infection any time your gecko has an injury.

number of other species of lizards, remains unclear. Infestations of red mites on crested geckos are unknown, but there is the possibility that they may contract this species from other reptiles.

Death and Euthanization

Should a death occur among your geckos, you should always do your best to determine the cause, especially if you own other animals that could be at risk. A freshly dead gecko should be examined all over to see if there are any clues to the cause of its demise. Things to look for include bite marks, skin tears, shedding problems, broken bones, blood or bloody feces in the cage, etc. Feel the abdomen for hard objects that may indicate egg binding or an

Salmonella and Your Gecko

This bacterial infection is more of a problem for reptile keepers than for the actual animals. It should be assumed that every reptile and supply used for reptiles is a potential source of *Salmonella*. The truth is that most reptiles do have *Salmonella* bacteria in their systems, and it is believed this bacteria is beneficial—or at least not harmful—to the animals. *Salmonella* is shed by reptiles through the feces.

Infections in humans usually cause diarrhea and fever, but can become more severe and even fatal for infants as well as those with a compromised immune system. All responsible reptile keepers will sanitize their hands immediately after handling reptiles and their supplies. Never eat or drink when handling reptiles or their supplies. Keep reptiles out of food preparation areas. Pregnant or nursing mothers should avoid contact with reptiles. Children handling reptiles should always be supervised by an adult, as well as taught about how to prevent the contraction of this illness. No matter how much your child loves your gecko, do not let him or her kiss it.

impaction. Try to find out if any chemicals were used in the vicinity of your reptiles.

A dark blue-green dot on the belly, appearing as if the skin has been stained, usually appears several hours after death. This dot is really just the bile leaking out of the gall bladder and absorbing into adjacent tissue, which is one of the earliest indications that decomposition has set in. It is not an indicator of the cause of death.

A gecko in the process of dying will sometimes open and close its mouth while lying on the floor of the cage, and often he will get a mouthful of substrate. Some keepers who find their dead gecko with substrate in his mouth may jump to the conclusion that he died due to ingestion of the substrate, but this is normally not the case.

It is obviously upsetting to lose a pet. It is even more upsetting to have to make the decision to euthanize a reptile that has no hope for recovery. A gecko with a terminal ailment should be humanely euthanized by a veterinarian before he unnecessarily suffers too much. Do not attempt euthanasia of your gecko yourself, as you are likely to cause your pet more suffering.

Necropsy

If you have an animal mysteriously die, you may want to know what happened. This is especially important if the gecko was kept in close proximity to other lizards that could possibly be at risk. If there are no clear external reasons for the death, and it is obviously not due to poor care on your part, then having your vet perform a necropsy will help determine the cause. A necropsy is a dissection of the animal to analyze his internal structures for abnormalities in search of the cause of death. In humans, we call this an autopsy.

The best subjects will be as fresh as possible. Since you should at least check on your geckos daily, you will notice when one dies. Immediately remove him from the cage and refrigerate him in an airtight plastic bag until you can deliver him to your vet. Do not freeze the gecko, as this may damage cellular structure and make diagnosis difficult in some circumstances. The chances of determining the cause of death is reduced with animals that are showing early stages of decomposition, yet prominent problems like impactions will still be easily seen.

Often, everything will visually appear normal, yet your vet may suggest having organ samples examined by a histopathologist, who will look for viruses, bacteria, and other pathogens on a cellular level. This is costly, yet a worthy investment if you have a large colony of reptiles that you want to protect.

Chapter 7

Other *Rhacodactylus* Species

After learning how fascinating crested geckos can be, the keeper may want to expand his collection with other members of the genus. Though the five other species of *Rhacodactylus* are not as commonly available as R. *ciliatus*, some are regularly available as captive-bred animals, though usually for a much higher price.

Rhacodactylus auriculatus

Commonly known as the gargoyle gecko, this species is second to the crested gecko as far as availability and price is concerned. It is also the best second choice *Rhacodactylus* species for someone who has mastered the keeping of crested geckos. The name refers to the grotesque appearance of the head, which has odd bony protuberances sticking up from the crown. Another descriptive common name sometimes used is the bumpy-headed gecko. This species has been captive bred in limited numbers for many years. Both hatchlings and adults are similar in size to crested geckos, and the care is nearly identical.

Gargoyle geckos are found on the southern part of Grand Terre. The species generally occupies a much drier, open habitat than the other species of *Rhacodactylus*. It seems to prefer areas of scrubby vegetation, characterized by low shrubs and sparse trees. It has also been found in transitional areas between primary forest and natural or man-made clearings. It is semi-arboreal, at home in the trees and shrubs, but can even be found traveling or resting on the ground.

Aside from the bony ridges on its head, the gargoyle gecko is different from the crested gecko in other ways. Gargoyles will lose their tail just as easily as their relatives, but unlike crested geckos, gargoyle geckos are able to regenerate their tail again and again. This species is often quarrelsome when kept in groups, and breeding behavior often results in lost tails. It almost seems that fighting, rough courtship, and tail autotomy is a natural part of this gecko's life. Upon close

R. auriculatus is called the gargoyle gecko because of the strange bony knobs on its head.

examination, regenerated tails don't always have the same color and scale pattern as the original, but from afar, a fully regenerated tail looks like the original. Unlike with crested geckos, owners don't need to worry about permanent tail loss if they want to keep a fully proportioned gecko on display.

As mentioned above, this species is prone to regular fighting, which may actually be just rough courtship. Usually this happens between male and female, with the female causing more damage to the male than vice versa. Normally, tail loss is the main resulting injury, though skin tears may also occur. These injuries heal fast, and usually don't require any assistance. Infection is always a possibility, but the risk is greatly reduced if kept in a clean cage with good air circulation.

Feeding

Though gargoyle geckos can be given the same cricket and fruit puree diet as crested geckos, they seem to prefer more crickets than fruit. A good feeding schedule would be to offer supplemented crickets two or three times a week, and fruit puree once a week.

Breeding

A well-fed gargoyle gecko will reach sexual maturity at about a year old. Breeding can be easily accomplished by following the same guidelines presented for crested geckos. Eggs are best incubated at in the upper 70°F range to low 80°F (25.6 to 27.2°C) range to end up with a good mixture of male and female hatchlings. This species is known to live in excess of 20 years in captivity.

Unlike cresteds, gargoyle geckos readily regenerate lost tails, which will be similar in length to the original.

Care of Hatchlings

Gargoyles Are Cannibals

A large gargoyle gecko will readily eat a smaller gargoyle gecko. If you are raising a group of hatchlings, you should maintain them in separate enclosures. Alternatively, you can raise them together and start separating them out once when you notice some are getting larger or smaller than the others. While the other *Rhacodactylus* species will also eat their own kind, *auriculatus* is especially apt to do so.

As with adults, hatchling and juvenile gargoyle geckos will fight if kept in group situations. Again, this normally results in tail loss, but stress becomes an issue as well in group cages. Those weaker animals that are outcompeted by the stronger geckos will not grow as quickly as the ones that end up getting more food. The stronger geckos will even eat the tails of the weaker geckos and will gradually end up growing much faster. Eventually, they will reach the point where they can then cannibalize the smaller geckos. To prevent this, close and regular monitoring of the group is required. Set up geckos only of identical size in a group cage, and keep it that way. Once some start lagging behind on growth, they will need to be set up in a cage of their own. Those that are clearly not growing as quickly, frequently losing tails, or just not looking well, will need to be separated out and set up individually so they can recover. A more efficient method for best growth and minimal loss is to raise hatchlings alone in their own cages, though this will take up more room.

Color and Pattern Varieties

Like crested geckos, gargoyle geckos come in a wide array of colors and patterns to choose from. All have a base color of white, light grey, light tan, to pale yellow and even reddish orange. There are many different combinations of these basic morphs, and new variations continue to be produced with ongoing selective breeding.

The reticulated or mottled phase is a commonly available morph that is variable in itself. Dark mottling over the lighter background color characterizes this pattern morph. Sometimes this mottling is uniform over the entire body, while in other instances the mottling is concentrated into bold or faded bands. The overall appearance of this morph blends in extremely well with rough, lichen-covered tree bark.

The striped morph has stripes that run the length of the back, from the base of the head down to the beginning of the tail. There is often a pair of stripes starting at the eyes and running down the sides, paralleling the central stripes. These stripes contrast to varying

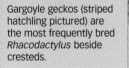

Gargoyle geckos (striped hatchling pictured) are the most frequently bred *Rhacodactylus* beside cresteds.

degrees with the background coloration. One gecko may even have some bold stripes running down the back and some more subtle stripes on the sides. Sometimes lateral striping is replaced by mottling.

The patternless morph is either devoid of patterning or has only insignificant amounts of darker patterning over the light base color. Some especially pale types are referred to as the ghost phase.

One particularly attractive morph is a rusty reddish-orange coloration that shows up as blotches or mottling in the reticulated morph and will be displayed as stripes in the striped morph.

Rhacodactylus leachianus

The giant gecko, *Rhacodactylus leachianus*, is the largest *Rhacodactylus* species, and the largest living gecko species. Large specimens grow to a total length of over 15 inches, though size is variable and averages slightly over 12 inches. About three-quarters of this total length is the gecko's stocky head and body, and one-quarter of this length is a seemingly disproportionate tail. The largest specimens weigh over a pound. There are two subspecies, *Rhacodactylus leachianus leachianus* from Grande Terre and *Rhacodactylus leachianus henkeli* from the Isle of Pines, located off the southern tip of Grande Terre. They live in primary rainforest habitats, and like all other *Rhacodactylus*, they are arboreal.

Subspecies

Suitable habitat on Grande Terre is very fragmented, with great expanses of separation between these areas. Different morphs have developed due to restricted genetics in these isolated areas. Aside from color and pattern differences, some of these morphs have body proportions distinctive from other types. Due to this, some morphs may even be considered additional subspecies. There is always controversy when assigning subspecific status to organisms, as the line drawn separating subspecific difference from regional variants is often unclear.

This *auriculatus* has nice red spotting. This species often has a lot of red and maroon in the pattern.

Of the two currently recognized subspecies, R. l. *leachianus* is larger and has a longer tail in relation to body size than R. l. *henkeli*. R. l. *leachianus*, also known as the Grande Terre giant gecko, encompasses other forms that might be separated out into additional subspecies as further research is conducted.

R. l. *henkeli*, known as Henkel's giant gecko, is restricted to the Isle of Pines and a number of other smaller islands. Populations on each island have differences from one another, and, like the Grande Terre giant gecko, some of these might be considered additional R. *leachianus* subspecies.

Vocal Giants

Both subspecies of *R. leachianus* are the most vocal of all the *Rhacodactylus* species. The sounds produced seem to be used as a form of communication between individuals, but sounds are also produced as a defensive measure. Sounds can range from rapid series of clucking noises when communicating with others to whistling noises when stressed. Rarely, growling noises have been heard.

Care

Captive care of giant geckos is along similar lines to that of crested geckos, but obviously you work on a larger scale for the adults. Like the crested geckos, this species will eat crickets and fruit puree, but it will also eat larger live items, such as pinky to fuzzy mice. In the wild, they have been known to eat small birds and other lizards. Cages should be at least 2 feet tall, but more space is always better. Tall, vertically oriented cages are preferable to wide, shallow enclosures.

Hiding places are a necessity with this species. In the wild, it has been found that this species is highly dependant on tree hollows for shelter and egg-laying sites. Unlike most other gecko species, pairs of *R. leachianus* seem to form relatively long bonds and will share tree hollows. Favored nesting hollows are repeatedly used. In captivity, artificial tree hollows should be provided, which can be created from

Giant geckos occur in two subspecies. This is *R. leachianus henkeli* from the Isle of Pines.

cork bark tubes of suitable size. These must be secured in an upright or diagonal position in the cage. If using a planted vivarium for housing giant geckos, choose sturdy plants that won't be crushed by the gecko's weight.

This species is very capable of inflicting a painful bite, but is not likely to attack if handled regularly. Bites may break the skin but are not as serious as bites from species such as tokay geckos.

Breeding

Since giant geckos form pair bonds, it is necessary to have a pair that is compatible. It may be frustrating to put together two mature giant geckos that you spent a lot of money on only to find that they dislike each other, ruining your hopes at breeding this species. After introducing a mature pair, closely monitor their reaction to each other over the next several days. If they are clearly not fighting, and spending the day together in the same cork bark round, they are most likely getting along and will be compatible.

An incompatible member of the opposite sex will have numerous bite marks on his or her

body, but don't confuse these signs of attack with scars sustained during normal courtship. When the male grasps the females behind the head with his mouth, sometimes marks are left on her neck. A rejected mate will not be allowed in the hollow and will appear stressed. As soon as you are clear that a gecko is not accepted by the intended mate, the gecko should be separated into a individual cage to recover from the ordeal. It is not recommended to try several females in the same cage with one male, unless the cage is very large and multiple artificial hollows are available in separate areas of the cage.

A nesting site must be provided. Since these geckos lay their eggs in tree hollows in the wild, similar concealed nesting sites are required. A section of a cork bark tube standing on end on top of a round plastic container filled with moistened vermiculite can work well. Deep buckets or other containers may also work well. Lidded plastic boxes with access holes cut in the lid may also be accepted by some individuals.

As with crested geckos, some breeders prefer to provide a cool rest period during the winter. Temperatures can be reduced to around 70°F (21.1°C), with temporary drops into the lower 60°F (16.7°C) range being acceptable. A cooling period may not be necessary for breeding stimulation, though it is recommended.

Giant geckos will lay multiple clutches over the course of the breeding season. Like all oviparous *Rhacodactylus* species, two eggs are normally laid per clutch. At least four clutches can be expected per season, assuming the female is well fed with properly supplemented food. Females will sometimes viciously defend their nest for several days after laying. Eggs may be incubated as described for crested geckos, and the duration of incubation is similar, if not slightly longer.

Care of Hatchlings

Hatchlings can be fed the same diet as adults, using fruit puree and properly sized crickets. As with most geckos, cages containing groups of hatchlings need to be regularly monitored for slight size discrepancies. Any gecko juveniles that aren't able to compete with the stronger individuals are likely to be stressed, and their health will deteriorate. When problems are identified early, the weaker geckos can be set up in their own enclosures to recover. Maintaining size consistency within cages of juveniles must be kept up with on a weekly basis until adulthood.

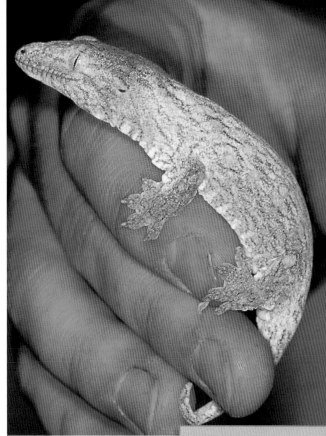

Even giant geckos start small. Successful captive breeding of this species seems to be increasing.

Hatchlings start out at about 4.5 inches (11.4 cm) total length, but this is variable depending on the variant or subspecies. Unlike other *Rhacodactylus* species, it takes well-fed giant geckos a long time to reach maturity. This can span two to four years, and differs depending on which type you have. Mature males can be recognized by their hemipenal bulges, though some forms of female giant geckos will have a bulbous tail base that can be mistaken for hemipenal bulges.

Species Comparison

Members of the genus *Rhacodactylus* have a lot in common with each other, yet each is unique in appearance, captive requirements, price, and availability. Some are better suited for beginners than others, and some have drawbacks that make them more suited for the advanced keeper. When choosing a species of *Rhacodactylus* for your next pet, use the following species comparisons to help in your decision making:

Rhacodactylus auriculatus the Gargoyle Gecko	*Pros:* Second to the crested gecko in terms of price, availability, color variation, ease of care and breeding. *Cons:* More aggressive in group setups than crested geckos, can inflict painful bites.
Rhacodactylus leachianus the Giant Gecko	*Pros:* Impressive size. Variable in color and appearance. *Cons:* Expensive, slow growing, can inflict painful bites, needs a large cage, difficult to breed.
Rhacodactylus sarasinorum	*Pros:* Unlike most other common types, this species will regenerate its tail if lost. Variable in color. *Cons:* Rarely available, expensive, fast moving.
Rhacodactylus chahoua	*Pros:* Tail isn't lost as easily as in other species. Tail will regenerate (but not to original size). Highly variable in color and pattern. *Cons:* Rarely available and expensive. Eggs difficult to hatch.
Rhacodactylus trachyrhynchus	*Pros:* Care and breeding similar to crested geckos. Interesting in that it gives birth to live young. *Cons:* Rarely available and expensive. Only produces one pair of babies per year, unlike the other species that can produce multiple clutches.

Some *R. sarasinorum* resemble the more common white-lined gecko of Indonesia and South East Asia.

Rhacodactylus sarasinorum

This species is known as Roux's giant gecko or the slender prehensile tailed gecko. It is found only in the southern part of Grand Terre. There it lives an arboreal existence high up in the rainforest trees. It grows to slightly over 10 inches (25.4 cm) in length and is the one member of the genus *Rhacodactylus* that superficially resembles the stereotypical gecko shape recognized by the general public. In fact, one color form closely resembles the white-striped or skunk gecko, *Gekko vittatus*.

Like all *Rhacodactylus*, this species is also highly variable in color and pattern, but not necessarily as widely variable as the other species. Usually a background coloration of reddish brown to tan to yellowish brown is present. Some specimens will be mottled with darker or lighter colors. Some otherwise monotonous individuals have white spots on the body, and another form has a pair of white stripes that extend from each eye diagonally back over the neck and joining together over the shoulders, forming a bold white V-shaped marking.

This gecko is much quicker and more unpredictable than other members of the genus. It rarely drops its tail, but if it does, it will regenerate. Care and breeding methods are as described for crested geckos.

The breeding of mossy giant geckos is still problematic, and many eggs fail to hatch.

Rhacodactylus chahoua

This species, known as the mossy giant gecko, is found on Grand Terre and the Isle of Pines. As its name implies, it has a coloration that effectively helps it blend in with moss and lichens that grow on the trunks and branches of the rainforest trees where it lives. Its pattern and coloration is highly variable, usually in shades of green, brown, rusty red, and gray-green, lichen color, but always has a mottled or banded camouflaging appearance. It grows to a total length of about 10 inches.

Care and breeding requirements are similar to that for the crested gecko. Well-cared-for hatchlings will reach adult size in one year. Like crested geckos, females will lay multiple clutches throughout the breeding season. Eggs are usually not buried as in the other species, and seem to have a more heavily calcified shell. Problems have occurred with the inability of hatchlings to successfully emerge from the thick eggshell, which can lead to the gecko dying in the egg if not helped soon enough.

Mossy giant geckos don't lose their tails as easily as other species. If one does, the tail rarely regenerates to anywhere near the original size.

Rhacodactylus trachyrhynchus

This species is known as the rough-snouted gecko due to the enlarged, domed scales located on the nose and extending up to the area between the eyes. There are two recognized subspecies. *R. trachyrhynchus trachyrhynchus* is found in the southern part of Grande Terre. It is the larger of the two subspecies,

The rough-snouted gecko is one of the few geckos that bears its young alive instead of laying eggs.

attaining a total length of 12 inches. The second subspecies, *R. trachyrhynchus trachycephalus*, occurs as an isolated population on a small island near Isle of Pines. It reaches a total length of around 9 inches.

This species has many features that are unlike those found in any other species of *Rhacodactylus*. Unlike all other members of the genus, this species is viviparous, giving birth to a pair of live young once a year. It also seems to have an affinity for water, and will voluntarily soak in the water bowl. This species also is capable of making sounds, and often vocalizes when kept in groups.

In addition to the presence of prominent hemipenal bulges in males, the sexes can often be told by the coloration. Males are normally dull brown with light-colored spots in paired rows running down the back. Females will have a lighter base color, with smaller spots. Coloration is variable and shouldn't be used as a reliable means of sexing rough-snouted geckos. Some may have faint darker banding or flecking over the entire body.

This species is rare in captivity, but a few breeders do work with both subspecies. Feeding, housing, and other aspects of captive care are similar to that described for the crested gecko. A large water bowl that the gecko can fit into should be provided to satisfy its love of water. Rough-snouted geckos will suffer from stress if not provided with hiding spots. Some individuals seem to like basking under lights, especially gravid females. After the neonates are born, they should be removed from the female's cage to prevent the possibility of cannibalism.

References

De Vosjoli, P., and Fast, F., and Repashy, A. 2003.
Rhacodactylus: The Complete Guide to Their Selection and Care.
Vista: Advanced Visions, Inc.

Seipp, R., and Henkel, F.W. 2000.
Rhacodactylus: Biology, Natural History, and Husbandry.
Frankfurt: Edition Chimaira.

CLUBS & SOCIETIES

Amphibian, Reptile & Insect Association

Liz Price
23 Windmill Rd
Irthlingsborough
Wellingborough NN9 5RJ
England

American Society of Ichthyologists and Herpetologists

Maureen Donnelly, Secretary
Grice Marine Laboratory
Florida International University
Biological Sciences
11200 SW 8th St.
Miami, FL 33199
Telephone: (305) 348-1235
E-mail: asih@fiu.edu
www.asih.org

The Global Gecko Association

c/o Leann Christenson
1155 Cameron Cove Circle
Leeds, Alabama 35094
E-mail: membership@gekkota.com
http://www.gekkota.com/

Society for the Study of Amphibians and Reptiles (SSAR)

Marion Preest, Secretary
The Claremont Colleges
925 N. Mills Ave.
Claremont, CA 91711
Telephone: 909-607-8014
E-mail: mpreest@jsd.claremont.edu
www.ssarherps.org

VETERINARY RESOURCES

Association of Reptile and Amphibian Veterinarians

P.O. Box 605
Chester Heights, PA 19017
Phone: 610-358-9530
Fax: 610-892-4813
E-mail: ARAVETS@aol.com
www.arav.org

RESCUE AND ADOPTION SERVICES

ASPCA

424 East 92nd Street
New York, NY 10128-6801
Phone: (212) 876-7700
E-mail: information@aspca.org
www.aspca.org

Petfinder.com
www.petfinder.org

Reptile Rescue, Canada
http://www.reptilerescue.on.ca/

RSPCA (UK)
Wilberforce Way
Southwater
Horsham, West Sussex RH13 9RS
Telephone: 0870 3335 999
www.rspca.org.uk

MAGAZINES

Herp Digest
www.herpdigest.org

Reptiles Magazine
P.O. Box 6050
Mission Viejo, CA 92690
www.animalnetwork.com/reptiles

WEB SITES

Gecko Network
http://www.geckonetwork.com/mainsec.htm

Gexfiles
http://www.gexfiles.com/

Herp Station
http://www.petstation.com/herps.html

Kingsnake.com
http://www.kingsnake.com

Melissa Kaplan's Herp Care Collection
http://www.anapsid.org/

Reptile Forums
http://reptileforums.com/forums/

The Reptile Rooms
http://www.reptilerooms.org/

Rhacodactylus Forums
http://www.pangeareptile.com/forums/index.php

Rhacodactylus Network
http://www.rhacodactylus.net

RhacRoom
http://www.rhacroom.com/forum/

Reptile Forums
http://reptileforums.com/forums/

Rhacodactylus ciliatus
http://www.rhacodactylus.net

About the Author:

Adam Black developed an intense interest in the natural world while growing up with the Florida Everglades nearly at his doorstep. He has kept and propagated numerous species of plants and animals throughout his life, which ultimately led to a career in the herpetological field. He currently manages the large gecko and colubrid breeding colonies at *The Gourmet Rodent, Inc.*, one of the largest commercial reptile breeding operations in the world. He lives in central Florida with his wife and son.

Photo Credits: